CW01082045

DANCE WITH LIFE

SAMANTHA HEANEY

TGH: THE GOOD HOUSE

Dance With Life

*I want to dedicate this book to my father,
John, who now watches over me every day and
became such a big part of this book.*

I love you dearly Dad.

CONTENTS

INTRODUCTION

Dear Reader,

First of all thank you for purchasing this book, Dance with Life; A collection of stories of being lost and found.

Throughout my own journey so far, there have been many moments where have I felt lost, but that gave me the opportunity to find myself, and then lose and find myself again and again.

Through this awareness, I have come to the conclusion that being lost isn't a bad thing and, really, being lost and found are both good. It's what makes life more of an adventure. I have also realised that I will never get to a destination point and that life will continue to unfold with some surprises along the way.

Throughout the stories in this book, you will feel an array of emotions; there's moments of joy, of sadness, grief, adventure and love.

At the end of each story, you will find a prescription; something you can do (act upon), think and feel, which you can choose depending on how you are feeling on that particular day. Or maybe some days you'll feel like diving into all of them.

There is also a journal prompt at the end of each story. Journaling has been such a therapeutic way for me to process what I am feeling. By asking myself prompt questions, I have been able to get out of my head and put my thoughts onto paper.

I wanted to give you a little taste of everything that may help you on your journey too.

I trust that this book will offer you some inspiration, hope, self-reflection, and some joyful moments as you journey through and perhaps offer a little TLC whenever you need it.

Samantha

1 MY JOURNEY HOME

EVERYTHING I AM SEARCHING FOR, IS ALREADY INSIDE OF ME

Here I am. I've arrived in another country. Although this time it isn't just to travel… I packed up and moved here. I have landed in Lisbon and something inside of me feels really overwhelmed. A sense of "Is this what I really want? What the F am I doing here? Am I meant to be here?" I feel fear creeping in and I feel very vulnerable, but there's also a sense of excitement and an openness to new opportunities, new friends and new adventures. Despite having been on a self-discovery journey for many years now, these emotions still surprise me and there's still a part of me that wants to disconnect from what I have labelled 'bad' emotions. Yet I must welcome it all and not run away from myself. It's just me and my dog, Bear. Going home now won't change anything.

So I decide to stay put and see what happens.

Since I was very young, I've lived away and had a real curiosity of exploring the world and seeing different places. I love the thrill and expansion I feel when I travel, when I meet different cultures and learn about different ways of living. I love the feeling I get when I go out in nature and hike in different places, connecting to the land wherever I am. So I definitely feel that adventure and travel is a part of me and is definitely a part of my soul. However, since arriving in Lisbon I've felt myself wondering, *Am I moving around just for that? Or am I running away from something, myself? Running away from certain things in my life?* I've found myself questioning, *what is it that I am seeking in other places? What is it that I seek that I feel I can't find in my home country, Scotland?* Was it just a desire for some adventure? Or, perhaps, it went a bit deeper than that.

When I sat with this final question, a couple of things came up for me that may be why I didn't feel at home in Scotland. The first one being connection. When I was younger, I didn't feel much connection with others and I felt I didn't really fit in. Somehow when I moved away it seemed easier to make friends that I could have a genuine connection with.

Another thing that I remembered was when I grew up in quite a small town and had thoughts like *"Is this it?"* as though I had this deep yearning for more, to see more; something about home just didn't do it for me.

I found myself questioning, *What if all I am seeking is already inside of me and everything else is just an extension from that?"*

As I witnessed all the emotions that arose since my arrival in Lisbon, it made me realise deeply, that I can't run away from myself. No matter where I am in the world, no matter where I go, I am still with me. I still have all the thoughts, the emotions, the feelings. It never goes away. I have had a huge realisation that home is me and, perhaps, I could find home in Scotland.

So, if home is me, can I find internal peace and happiness? Anchor deeply within and from this grounded space, then explore the world, but from a place of curiosity and adventure rather than running away from anything.

So much awareness crept up for me here in Lisbon, reflecting back on all the times I have been seeking happiness, joy and acceptance externally. Yes, to some extent I can find those things through experiences, but the true essence of it all is feeling that inside of me. Lighting up my world from the inside, and then allowing that light to shine outside.

Something about Lisbon has awoken something inside of me and although I've felt lost and uncertain, I feel I am also finding myself. Once again I've been called to surrender, to trust and go with the unknown.

It was during this time that I decided to write this book and share many stories of being lost and found. It's where the idea and creation of this book began.

So, let's dive into a journey of being lost and found but with an open mind that it really is okay to be lost and found, and then lose and find yourself again and again. To immerse yourself in it all.

Do: I invite you to take a moment and close your eyes. Take a few deep breaths into your belly and exhale out through your mouth. With each exhale imagine you are coming home to yourself, to your body and relaxing into the present moment. After a few minutes, open your eyes and come back into the room.

Feel: What does 'at home' feel like for you? Is it something inside or outside of you? What emotions come up for you when you feel at home?

Think: Can you think of a time where you felt at home? What memories come up for you?

Journal Prompt: Can you remember a time where you felt lost in your life? How did you get through it?

MY REFLECTION

DATE   /   /

2 GRIEF STRICKEN

OPENING TO GRIEF, IS OPENING TO LOVE

"Dad is dead" I hear down the phone. I am shocked to my core. Is this real? It can't be. They must have it wrong. I ask again, "Are you sure?" How can this be? It is real. I burst into tears and my heart breaks open, more than it ever has before. I come off the phone and in an instant I feel my whole life has been turned upside down. My head is running with so many thoughts. I need to get home now, but I also have to sort out how I do that... how to get me and my dog back home asap. I walk out to the terrace and I crash to the ground. Another layer of tears wash down my face. "Dad, are you there?" I ask. I look up to the sky and it's a beautiful sunny day. I just can't believe this is happening.

Grief hit me hard. Never did I think that this would become a huge part of my book. When I started this book, which wasn't long before I was hit with grief, I really thought that my parents would always be around. I never worried much about losing them suddenly and so early on. The thought did cross my mind from time to time, especially when you hear of other stories from people around you, but I never really thought it would happen to me. I guess it made me realise I had a bit of denial around death.

I've never experienced anything like it. My heart feel so broken and heavy and, with it being so sudden, I feel the shock of it all. It feels like heartbreak but 100 times more intense. I feel like someone is punching my heart again and again. Suddenly my whole world is turned upside down and I find myself having to pack up and move back to Scotland from Lisbon. I'd been living in Lisbon for almost 5 months, still finding my way, and then in an instant it all changed. My whole life changes and will never be the same as it was before.

That day still ignites something inside of me, the day I received the news. It was a typical Sunday chilling in my apartment when I heard. "Dad is dead." He was hit by a car on his bike and died at the scene. At first I didn't want to believe it; it couldn't be true. I found my mind thinking, *maybe it's a mistake, maybe they have it wrong.* I felt such deep shock and sadness. I felt so lost. Being in another country hearing this news just made it so much more challenging. I felt panic arise inside of me and wanted to run away. The week following that news was a blur. I had to wait 4 days until I could fly home due to having my dog with me. I have no idea how I got through those days and got myself and my dog on the flight. It was like something inside of me went into operation mode, getting everything fixed and organised to get home.

I found myself calling friends and telling them what happened. The more I shared the news, the more I felt a sense of understanding and it becoming more real. I had moments where I thought, *Okay, this is real*, and then moments of complete shock and bursting into tears. I sobbed so much and I still do now. I still have days where it really hits me and I feel the heartache.

I remember walking with Bear through Lisbon on autopilot and just crying down the streets. I didn't care who saw me or looked at me, my heart just wanted to mourn and open. My dog was my anchor during those first few days. I'd take him to the park every day and sit whilst he would run around. It helped me get outside and get some fresh air.

Once again I found myself so lost and unsure about life. I found myself speaking out loud to my dad and hoping he would connect with me. I do believe I received signs from him. Even in those early days, I felt he was around me and watching over me.

As I write this, it's been four months since my dad passed. I miss him dearly every day. It still F*-ing hurts. I've moved through so many different emotions; anger, pain, guilt, sadness. There's also been joy and a deep sense of love as I allow myself to remember all the good times we had too.

I've learned a lot about grief and that it can come in many different forms. Through grief therapy, one of the exercises I did was to reflect on my life and write down a history of losses. Through doing this I noticed that I had experienced quite a lot of loss. From relationships, to moving houses quite a few times, loss of pets and loss of people too. I feel that from reflecting on this, I've noticed patterns of fear of commitment throughout my life and that it could possibly be why I moved around a lot and why I've never committed to anything long term. It's definitely been an eye opener to me and something I am still discovering more about.

My journey with grief so far has been somewhat an interesting experience as, although initially it was the death of my dad, it has also opened up so much more about my past and the relationship I've had with myself over the years. It has brought so much more awareness to how I've been operating in the world.

I believe that although my dad isn't here physically anymore, he is with me, always. He is an angel watching over me and he is helping guide me through each day now. I connect with him every day. He's shown me more signs that he is around. I feel in time he will be my fuel to push through fear. To live my life more fully and freely. To have more love and compassion towards myself and others. To do more of the things I love now and not to wait for tomorrow, next week, next month. To use him as a reminder of how precious life is.

Human existence is a gift and if I can allow myself to see the beauty in everything and have an open mind, I can truly have a joyful and fulfilling life. Of course I will still miss him and feel pain and sadness that he isn't here anymore. I'll miss the physical form of him. I accept that perhaps I may never be fully content that he isn't here anymore and that there will be many more times when I will think of him and be reminded that I will not see him physically again, and that hurts so much. I also know how important it is for me to keep opening my heart and not shut off from this; to allow all the emotions that want to be felt, be felt and that the more I do this, the more I can feel love.

You see, when we allow ourselves to feel the whole spectrum of emotions, and that includes anger, pain, shame, guilt, sadness and grief, we also open ourselves up to feel more love, joy, expansion and happiness. This journey with my dad is certainly showing me that more deeply than ever before.

Do: If you have lost someone and would like to connect with them, I invite you to find a space where you can be alone and feel relaxed. Sitting down comfortably, gently close your eyes and start to think of the person you have lost. Bring them into your awareness, and imagine you are sitting down in front of them. Let them know how much you love them and give them a hug.

Feel: How did that person make you feel? What memories come up for you? If you haven't lost someone physically, perhaps you have lost a pet you loved, or a relationship you loved. Welcome in the feelings you felt when they were around.

Think: Think of a special memory you hold of that person, pet or relationship… What do you remember?

Journal Prompt: If you could open yourself more to love, how would your life change?

MY REFLECTION

DATE   /   /

3 PANDEMIC LIFE

LIFE IS UNPREDICTABLE AND THE MORE I LET GO OF CONTROL, THE MORE I AM IN FLOW

"Stay at home. You can't go more than 5 miles from where you live". This is real. For a while I don't think much of it and think it will all pass but it hasn't. Lock-down is officially here. I am feeling a mix of emotions. Part of me is thinking this could be nice to slow down and reflect a bit. Another part of me is a little unsure.

At the start of lockdown I really enjoyed it; moving slower, being back at home and appreciating the small things I had missed, like walks along the beach and spending a lot of time with my family. Now, after what's happened with my dad, I am truly grateful for all the memories that we shared and the time we had 'off' that allowed us to go for many walks together and reflect on our life journeys. I feel that through our time together, our bond became stronger and we became so much closer.

I spent a bit of time getting creative and created my first online course '*Living in Alignment with your Menstrual Cycle*'. This was a really enjoyable experience to pull together and help women go through this journey to develop a better understanding of their body and their cycle - something that had been a huge part of my healing journey.

Also, I felt challenged throughout the last couple of years as I was still transitioning to life back home after my time in Saudi. I'd lived there almost five years and overall it was an incredible experience. I grew as a person a lot whilst living there, and I feel that's where my journey really started with myself. Being back home was bringing up a lot of old stories and beliefs I had about myself and I found myself sometimes feeling like the younger girl I was before I left. I sometimes felt out of place, like I didn't fit in here anymore and questioned moving back and asking myself if I had I done the right thing. It was this sense of going backwards.

As time went on and we moved into a 2nd and then a 3rd lockdown, I definitely had days of feeling really overwhelmed. That feeling of uncertainty, loss of control, and all my trips being cancelled one by one. For someone who loves to travel, this was a big shock to the system! It made me really see that life is unpredictable and to really honour each day and live life to the full as much as possible, in each and every moment, and to not get too attached to any outcomes. That's definitely still a work in progress.

More than anything, I deeply missed face-to-face connection. I loved being around people, sharing through heart-to-heart conversations, having hugs, laughing, dancing and going on adventures together. I missed that so much. I had days where I felt okay and days where I felt so isolated. Even having my family around me, I still felt that.

I found myself turning to food more, for comfort. I felt like I had no control of what was going on. I have many different practices and tools that really help me come into my body, to relax and de-stress, which has been a blessing during these times. However, my relationship with food has always been a challenging one, like a love/hate relationship. It's definitely something I turn to, even when I am excited or happy.

During the pandemic, I healed a lot within my ancestral lineage. At times, I felt very triggered being back at home and it definitely tested me and mirrored parts of myself that I still felt disconnected to. However, through some deeper work and healing practices with a few mentors, I feel I've found more peace with my family. I feel grateful to have had the time to move through this and to have more of an understanding of certain dynamics within my family.

Pandemic life also brought me to Lisbon, which is funny when I think about it; I'd heard of Lisbon but it had never been on my radar to go and visit there. However, last year through a couple of conversations with friends and hearing good things, I decided to book a flight last minute and took a trip over for a week (which turned into 7 weeks!)

When I arrived, I instantly felt good vibes, a nice energy, and I met some lovely people. The beautiful blue skies and lovely weather also helped and I found myself thinking "I could live here!!"

Fast forward 6 months and it happened, but little did I know all that would happen to me during my time in Lisbon. As much as I feel my whole life was turned upside down, I am also grateful for it and truly believe that everything happens for a reason, no matter how painful or uncomfortable it may be.

This somewhat surreal time of living on earth, which is still with us as I write this, has certainly been a journey for me and I am sure for any of you reading this book. I definitely have had moments of feeling lost and uncertain, but also found myself in many ways and continue to do so on this ever-changing journey of self-discovery. It has taught me that life is unpredictable and to learn to let go of control and be more in natural flow with life. The more that I can trust and surrender, the more I can enjoy the journey and whatever may come my way.

Do: Life is unpredictable. With this uncertainty, I invite you to do something today that brings you joy. Carve out some time for you to have fun, be playful and just be in the moment. Perhaps it is art, singing, dancing, music or being in nature. You do you!

Feel: As we moved into the pandemic, what feelings arose for you?

Think: What has been your overall experience of living during these times?

Journal Prompt: Have you experienced a time in your life where life felt unpredictable and something happened out of your control? What happened, and how did you get through it?

MY REFLECTION   **DATE**   /   /

4 A DEEPER AWAKENING
THROUGH THE DARKNESS, THERE IS LIGHT

It is the midst of the pandemic and I'm moving through a lot; ancestral healing, womb healing and connecting more to my feminine energy. It's deep, dark, uncomfortable at times, but also beautiful and healing. I am shedding away layers of myself to bring me back home to my truth. I am opening myself up to the shame, the guilt, the rage, the anger, all that I have suppressed for so long. I am noticing that as I open more, I am feeling more love, acceptance, pleasure and joy. I am starting to feel my body and my heart.

Looking back, I feel this journey started when I decided to come off The Pill and give my body a break from it, allowing a normal cycle to resume. Little did I know what would evolve from that intuitive idea and where it would bring me today. I've slowly, very slowly, been shedding away the layers to come back home to my body and to my truth. Becoming my own best friend, understanding my needs, my desires and who I truly am. Having acceptance of the shame, guilt and resentment I felt for many years; that deep rooted feeling of not being enough or loveable. Beginning to be open and vulnerable with myself.

I developed a deep understanding that I have so much wisdom inside of me and to learned to connect with myself more deeply and lovingly, from an embodied way rather than a mindful way. Not needing to seek validation or approval from others, not putting others before myself and letting go of 'people-pleasing' and doing things I don't really want to do. I moved through a lot of ancestral healing on both my mother's side and father's side and did a lot of womb healing which has allowed me to connect more with my feminine energy, my intuition and to Mother Earth. Throughout this journey, I realised how often I'd been lost in my mind, overthinking, doubtful and how it consumed me in many different areas of my life. Once I started to unravel and connect more to my body, my heart and my womb, I found so much more depth in myself and began to feel so much more.

I've worked with a lot of different tools and practices; Cognitive Behavioural Therapy (CBT), Hypnotherapy, Counselling, Reiki, Life Coaching, Meditation, the list goes on. All have been so incredibly helpful in their own individual ways, but what I've discovered is the power of coming more into my body through embodiment practices, such as breathwork, sound and movement. Releasing trapped emotions from my body, letting go of old wounds, giving myself so much tender love and self-care. This has been truly transformational for me over the last couple of years. These techniques about which I feel excited and passionate, I share with others on their own journeys through my coaching and healing work. Of course, it's an ongoing journey for me too, but I feel the deeper I go, the deeper I can take others in very loving and safe way.

This journey so far has taught me to have healthy boundaries in place and to honour my needs. That it's okay to fill up my own cup first, before I go out into the world. That I am deserving of taking time with myself and my body and that it's safe to slow down. I don't have to be on the go all the time and it's important for me to have more balance with my feminine and masculine energy, which is essentially being vs. doing.

I realised how much I had been attached to the doing, 'go-go energy' and how tired my body was. I spent time looking at myself in the mirror, saying sorry for all the things I'd said and done that were hurtful, and reminded myself that I was always just trying to do my best. I also feel this journey has allowed me to be much more connected to my emotions and that each and every one of them is welcome and sacred. Allowing myself the safety and space to move into anger, fear, or shame and allowing my body to feel it all without any judgement. It's actually very healthy to do so. The more I've allowed myself to feel this spectrum of emotions, I've noticed how much more I can feel joy, pleasure and freedom to just be me. All of me.

Do: Spend some time today to notice where in your life you are moving from your mind vs. your heart. Notice how different it feels when you make a decision from your heart.

Feel: Do you feel comfortable expressing all your emotions? What emotions do you find challenging to feel?

Think: Think of a time where you did something enjoyable that was just for you.

Journal Prompt: Imagine waking up every day and honouring yourself first before going out into the world, how different would your life look and how would your life change?

MY REFLECTION

DATE   /   /

5 SAUDI ARABIAN ADVENTURES

TRUE GROWTH COMES FROM THE MORE CHALLENGING AND UNCOMFORTABLE TIMES

Wow, is this really happening? I am embarking on a plane to start a new chapter in Saudi Arabia to work as a Personal Assistant for an oil and gas company. I feel excited, nervous, unsure and curious. As I get settled on the plane, I have met another couple of women who are also moving there. We share some wine together and speak about how we are feeling - mixed emotions but excited to step into the unknown.

So, how did it happen? One day, whilst sitting at the desk in my job prior to this move, I was having a nosy online to see what was out there, anything that took my interest. During this phase of my life I had a deep desire to travel and I remember thinking, I will save for a year, quit my job and make it happen. I then saw the opportunity to live and work in Saudi, and I had the experience they were looking for, so decided to apply 'just for the fun of it'.

That same day I received a phone call being invited to go for an interview in London. At first I was startled and, honestly? I thought it was too good to be true as they advised that they would pay for my flight to London and also reimburse me for an overnight stay in a hotel. I said yes and after the call immediately called my dad to explain what had happened and also checked out the company website to see it was all legit. The rest, I guess, is history. Within a few months, I got offered the job, packed up my things, sorted a visa and moved to the Middle East.

Then BOOM. It hit me. I had arrived. It felt strange and I a little uncomfortable. In the airport as we moved through customs I felt nervous. I felt a little scared too. My emotions were all over the place. It was such a different environment, witnessing many women covered up in hijabs and abayas and hearing a different language. Living and growing up in a small town, it opened up my eyes. We were met after customs and collected our luggage and were then driven to the compound where we were living. As we drew closer and arrived at the entrance, I witnessed guards, men standing with guns, and thought to myself, *Wow, I've never seen a gun in person before!* They checked us in and I arrived safely at the house I'd be sharing with another woman for a few months until my apartment was ready to move into.

That next day I felt overwhelmed, and I felt very vulnerable. I found myself thinking, *What have I done? Is it going to be okay?* I felt so out of my depth. I have a tendency to do these things; I sign up like "Yes, let's do it" but then it hits me later.

I didn't know it as much then, but I now understand how intense and how much of an impact it has on us when we move, especially to another country. I called home and spoke to my family, sharing my thoughts and feelings. I then ventured out to explore a little and try to find my surroundings. It was bloody roasting! I'd never felt heat like it before. I arrived in June, so Summer was in full swing. It was a dry heat, so not as bad as humidity, but still the intensity of it felt like my eyes were burning.

As I write this, something has come up that I want to share with you. As I was going through the process of moving to Saudi, I experienced my first panic attack. Looking back I can see it all happening so clearly now, although not at the time.

You see, I have a tendency of not fully expressing how I feel, as so many of us do I guess. The persona of having it 'all together', always saying I was 'good' when in fact maybe I was not so good. Putting on the mask to face the external world we live in. On the lead up to this move, so many emotions were stirring inside of me, but I didn't know how to fully express them. I just kept going along day by day, kind of aware that I was feeling excited, nervous and unsure at times, but not fully having those conversations with those around me.

In response, my body went into overdrive and the panic attack took place. I was at work when it happened. I suddenly felt weird; my hands went all clammy. I felt like my vision was out of sorts too. I remember thinking "I need to get to the toilet and just be on my own", unaware of what was happening. I reached the bathroom and my heart was racing. I felt like I couldn't breathe and I went into panic. One of my colleagues came into to check on me to try and help me relax. Once I felt like it had passed, I burst into tears. I felt a huge release of emotion move through me. I guess it was the build of everything that was going in internally and without me fully realising it, I'd hit the peak and my body released through this panic attack. It was a pretty scary experience, especially as at the time I didn't know what was happening to me.

Through a conversation with my mum she confirmed what I had experienced. I had a couple more panic attacks following that day, not right away as such, but throughout my journey in Saudi over the following years to come. I wanted to share this as maybe you are reading this and have also experienced this in your life. You aren't alone. I believe so many of us feel stuck and feel scared to express our emotions, especially the ones we've labelled 'bad' and it can feel pretty scary to be vulnerable and to show fear. Personally, this has been one of the most liberating things I've done through my own journey - learning to face all my emotions. To feel them all and to give them space to be heard, seen and move through me.

It took me around 6 months before I began to settle more into life in Saudi. The culture was a bit of a shock and it took me time to adjust in this new way of living. Living on a compound with other expats definitely helped and I made (and still have) amazing friends who live there. Sometimes I felt like I was in a little bubble, unaware of what was happening in the world, just getting on with life in this new environment.

Things I think about now when I look back and laugh, are all the times I went shopping to buy clothes, to then go back to my apartment to try them on (there were no changing rooms) hoping they were okay and they weren't then having to get a bus back to return them. Although, I later discovered a couple of toilets within the shopping mall where I was able to try things on, so it saved that extra journey!

I also felt frustration from not being able to drive, so it was challenging to do things spontaneously. I'd have to call a driver to come and collect me, sign them in at the entrance to the compound at the gate, to then make the journey.

I spent three months in Saudi before my first trip to Bahrain. Freedom! I experienced my first brunch and what a laugh we had. This was one of the first times I felt more settled in Saudi. I was beginning to find routine, meet some lovely friends and explore not just Saudi, but other countries.

Another thing that I found challenging, was how honest and direct the culture was. They really said it as it was. Some funny examples were, I'd go into work on a Sunday morning, perhaps after an eventful weekend, and be told how tired I looked. Did I not sleep well? Even the boss I had there was very direct and kind of scared me at times, like an authority type figure. I found it really challenging at times because it sometimes felt like an attack, but it wasn't really. It was just triggering something inside of me that felt uncomfortable and, being totally honest, back then I felt scared to speak back, to speak my truth and to stand up for myself.

In Saudi it was also a very unpredictable way of working, things would always change last minute so I had to become more adaptable and let go of the need to know/of control, and essentially go with the flow.

I was 26 when I moved there. Still so young and open to the world. Over the first couple of years I partied a lot and I explored so many different countries, some of which I will share with you in this book. It really opened my eyes. I loved experiencing different cultures, hearing people's stories and experiences. I loved feeling like I was expanding and everywhere I went felt so different and alive in its own unique, beautiful way. Me and my friends had so much fun. Music, dating, sightseeing, brunches, no care in the world. Literally living for each weekend. I wasn't fulfilled in my work at all, but the pay check and the trips away made it worthwhile… for some time anyway.

When I first decided to go to Saudi, my main drive was money. When I found out what my salary would be and that I would be in the middle of the world, which would allow me to travel more, it was a no brainer. However, what I didn't realise was that this was the start of an incredible journey of self-discovery and my life was going to change so much, in so many ways. Even as I write this, tears fall down my face as I feel it deep in my soul. I see now how much I have grown and how I have come back home to myself.

Do: Do something today outside of your comfort zone. Make that phone call, apply for that job, try a new gym class. Whatever you have been thinking about doing but feel fear creeping in, see if you can lean into it and take aligned action.

Feel: How do you feel when challenges come your way? Is it something you find easy to face and step into, or do you feel you want to run away?

Think: The next time something challenging comes your way and you feel fear, ask yourself what's the worst thing that could happen? Sometimes the thought of something is more fearful than the actual experience - it's just our ego trying to protect us and keep us safe.

Journal Prompt: Can you recall a memory where you felt challenged but, through that challenge, you grew? Journal on your experience.

MY REFLECTION   DATE   /   /

6 A FEELING OF DISCONNECT

THE MORE I CONNECT TO MYSELF, THE MORE I FEEL AT HOME WITH ALL PARTS OF MYSELF

"How are you Sam?" "Yeah I'm good, you?" Once again I have found myself saying I'm 'good' when actually, I'm not okay. I'm sad. I'm fed up. I just can't bring myself to say the truth; I don't want to come across negative or a burden, so I will just pretend that I am okay.

———

As I reflect on my life and journey so far, I can see how often I was living from my head and how I have experienced anxiety throughout my life. I've have moments of feeling so exhausted from thinking; worrying about life, not doing enough, what other people thought of me, wanting to fit in and just an overall feeling that I was not enough how I was.

I can see now how disconnected I was to my body and my emotions. I'd put on the brave face, always be smiling, when inside sometimes I felt a lot of pain and sadness. I didn't know how to express these emotions. I'd feel guilty if I got angry about certain things, like it wasn't a 'good look' to express in that way. I carried a lot of shame.

I also didn't feel good about the way I looked. Growing up, when I was a teenager, I developed acne and felt very self-conscious about my skin and I didn't feel pretty. I felt incredibly visible and in a way that I didn't like. I compared myself to other girls and always wanted more, as though the way I was, wasn't enough. I developed a story that to be accepted, or to fit in, was based on the way I looked and not about the values or the person I was.

I truly believe that this is why I developed a hormonal imbalance. I was disconnected to my power and to my life-force energy. I was disconnected from my womb and heart. I believe this is why a lot of women have menstrual issues, because there's a disconnect to the body and a feeling of not being enough.

I felt scared to fully let people in, scared of being hurt or rejected. I didn't feel loveable or even worthy of love. I'd give myself and my energy to other people, wanting to fit in and be accepted, especially men. I'd allow other people's thoughts to consume me and believed them to be true. I was always on the go and didn't know how to rest, or even that resting and slowing down was an option. Over the years I wasn't aware of any of this, it was just a subconscious and reactive way of my being.

However, as I began my journey of self-discovery and started to inquire more into my ways of being, this feeling of disconnect grew stronger and my awareness was beginning to unravel. I began to question areas of my life and wonder, *Is this what I want? Does this feel in alignment with who I desire to be?* I was starting to see why I felt this way and I wanted to change the story. I wanted to feel more connected to my body and not feel shame around her. I wanted to give myself more love and compassion and start to put my needs first. I wanted to feel the love that I'd been seeking in other places. I wanted to feel enough. I was beginning to see that in order to live life this way, it started with my internal world… it started with me.

Do: I invite you to spend time today to rest. Even if it's just a few minutes, connect to your breath and notice how it feels to be in stillness and do nothing. Just be with yourself.

Feel: Do you feel connected to your body? What emotions arise for you when you think about your relationship with your body? Without any judgement, just notice.

Think: Are you always on the go and struggle to slow down? How does that impact your day-to-day life?

Journal Prompt: Imagine you feel so connected to your body and your intuition, that you always make decisions from your inner space... what does your life look and feel like from this space?

MY REFLECTION
DATE   /   /

7 HELLO HORMONAL IMBALANCE

MY BODY CAN HEAL NATURALLY WHEN I GIVE HER THE ATTENTION AND SPACE TO DO SO

I'm coming off The Pill. I want a break from it, I tell myself. But as I say yes to this decision, I am also so nervous of doing so. What if my skin gets worse? Can I handle that? I know deep down it's the right thing to do… I must trust. Little do I know what's to unfold.

———————

I'd been on The Pill for many years, more so to help maintain my acne (which actually didn't really help!), but I was too scared to come off it incase it made it worse. I'd also had a course of specific medication previously to help my skin as nothing else I had tried had really worked. Coming off The Pill did have a positive impact for me and my skin cleared up dramatically. However, I wouldn't recommend taking this route without feeling it's the right thing for you and speaking to your doctor regarding the side effects that can occur. I was also at a point in my life where I was really looking after my health, so it felt like a good time to have a break from The Pill and see what happened. Fast forward a year and I still didn't have a period. How strange.

Although I didn't think there was anything to worry about, my friend was concerned and advised me to go get checked out. Still oblivious to anything being wrong as such, I agreed and went to see a gynaecologist. I was booked in for a scan and was told that I had a hormonal imbalance called PCOS. I was in shock. I'd never heard of it before and asked more about it. The response was that there were multiple cysts in my ovaries and the best thing to do was to go back on The Pill and that would help regulate my cycle and get my period back.

This didn't sit well with me. I began to question, *why isn't my body working the way it naturally should? What is PCOS? Is there anything I could do naturally to reverse the symptoms?* I refused to go back on The Pill and my journey to reversing PCOS began.

I began researching and understanding more about hormonal imbalances and the causes of them. PCOS is quite a tricky one as it can have many different symptoms and reasons for cause and a lot of the time it is underlying and goes undiagnosed. Many women don't even know they have PCOS, like myself. I reckon I had it for many years as I had other symptoms but didn't connect it all until I'd come off the pill.

The first thing I dived into was working with a nutritionist who specialised in helping women with PCOS. I was given a three-month protocol on how to eat, supplements to take and I also had some extensive blood work taken to understand what was going on inside my body. Over the three months, I cut out all processed foods, caffeine and alcohol. I had a high protein diet and ate lots of veggies and fibre to help eliminate any excess hormones and toxins. I also wanted to understand more about the menstrual cycle and found myself drawn to books that shared insights about the cycle and what our bodies go through each month.

Wow. It totally opened my eyes to how I had been living, so on the go go go and never allowing my body to slow down and rest. I saw my bleed as a burden, something that was a nuisance and was so glad for it to be over but what I was discovering was the power in it and how amazing it is. The first book I read was like my bible and something I still go back to from time to time. I began to learn about the different seasons; like the seasons we have each year, we also have this through our cycle. The rise in energy during the first half of the cycle and depletion in energy during the second (hello pre-menstrual). I also learned about different foods to eat depending on where I was within my cycle and how to track my cycle each month.

I was blown away with this wisdom and knowledge and began to look at my cycle as an opportunity to be reborn each month. I could start again, set new intentions, get creative, show myself to the world and share whatever was alive in me, and then retreat, slow down and reflect on the journey and let go of what wasn't serving me.

I also began to look at the way I was training my body. Before, I was working out 5-6 days per week, even during my bleed, and was left feeling exhausted and fatigued. Now I was beginning to check where I was at in my cycle and where my energy levels were and plan according to that to help my body move in a way that would support her rather than exhaust her. I was beginning to find a new way of living and it really excited me.

During my second time in Thailand, I met a Reiki Master and decided to get my first attunement to allow me to become a Reiki Practitioner. I wanted to work with the energy body and bring my body back to balance, not just physically, but also mentally and spiritually.

Another dear friend in Saudi helped me with Acupuncture and Reiki Healing and I believe this had a profound effect on bringing my body back to it's natural state of being. I also looked at any stress in my life and ways to manage it, through yoga, meditation and beginning a morning practice before starting my day.

Slowly but surely over time, my bleed began to become regular again. When I got my first bleed following coming off The Pill, I cried with so much gratitude. My body was beginning to respond to all that I was doing to help her.

Over the next year or so, I'd have a bleed, then miss the next month, then bleed and then miss again, but slowly my bleed became every month and I now have a healthy bleed every month. I recently got a Dutch Test done which I highly recommend if you want to get an overall understanding of your hormones and it also includes stress hormones too. I was delighted with the results. Everything is in balance and I had another moment of deep gratitude for my body as I truly believe that all I have done to help support her and continuing to keep coming home to myself and trusting myself, has led me to bringing my body back to harmony. What also made me smile was knowing that with everything in balance, it means that (all being well) when I decide that I'd like to conceive a child, I know that my body will be able to carry and support it.

It's funny; sometimes things happen to you and in that moment you can feel like, *WHY?!* But I truly believe that everything that happens to us is a blessing, even the things that cause us pain. We can learn from it, evolve from it and grow from it. Asking ourselves, *what is the lesson in this? What is thing doing for me rather than to me? How can I be with this and understand it?* For me, I am grateful for PCOS, for my body showing me that I was out of balance and to check in with her. To listen to her, honour her and give her the love and support she deeply needed. It's an ongoing journey and in no way am I perfect, I still have my moments, I still question things, I still overthink and feel anxious sometimes, but there is so much more kindness, compassion and self-awareness towards myself.

Do: Start tracking your cycle every day, to record how you are feeling emotionally, mentally and physically. This will give you a deeper understanding of your body and your energy levels. You can start to see patterns of times where you may need some down time, extra self-care and you can start to carve this in your diary as a way to support your body and all she is moving through every day.

Feel: How do you currently feel about your cycle? Is it something you enjoy or something you find difficult?

Think: Can you remember a time where you gave your body the permission to slow down and rest, and from that space it brought your body back into a state of balance?

Journal Prompt: If you gave yourself permission to honour more self-care and prioritise your needs first, how would this impact your life?

MY REFLECTION

DATE   /   /

8 THAILAND ADVENTURES

THE MORE I STEP INTO ADVENTURE, THE MORE I EXPERIENCE JOY AND FREEDOM

Hello Thailand. We have landed. Wow, it's absolutely beautiful. The beaches, the sand, the warm sun on my face, I feel so excited to be here. Nine days island hopping with a group of people. Seven days in a juicing retreat to detox the body. What could possibly go wrong?

We partied, we danced and we experienced our first full moon party, which are very well known in Thailand. The full moon took place on the final night of our island hopping adventure and the next day it was time to travel to the retreat we would be staying at for the duration of the holiday. I did not think this part through when booking the trip. Before we went on the trip I had looked into how we would get from the final island to Phuket and the plan was to get a flight there. However, when we got to Thailand and I looked into sorting flights, there were none available. I then looked into other options and it looked like it wasn't going to be too much of a journey so I was pretty confident about it all. This journey ended up being 8 hours long, involving a tuk tuk, boat, bus and taxi. I think my friend literally wanted to kill me by the end of it. Having only had a few hours sleep following the full moon party and a little hungover, this trip to Phuket felt like the longest and horrific thing ever. At one point we thought we were going to be kidnapped and never see our family again as we saw a few signs for Phuket and the driver going the opposite direction. Denise kept saying to me "I have a bad feeling about this, something doesn't feel right!"

I tried my best to remain calm, but I was also feeling uncertain myself and praying that we would arrive in one piece, safe and sound. Thankfully that did happen and after a long tiring day we arrived at the retreat.

I remember us arriving at the retreat and they just looked at us like, *What do we have here?!* I literally felt like shit. Exhausted, hungover and certainly not at all ready to be diving into a retreat. One of our friends was also at the retreat and had been there for a few days already and looked so bright and fresh and I felt like death's door. The first few days were hard, I won't lie. I felt irritable and thought *Why am I here?!* The detox process was intense, having ate and drank for 9 days and then going into a raw food, juice cleanse wasn't our brightest idea. As my body began to detox all the toxins, I felt exhausted, had a sore head and just wanted to be anywhere but there.

However, by the end of the retreat we felt great and so refreshed. It felt good to get some goodness in me again and allow my body to rest from the fun trip. We lounged at the pool, chatted about the experience we were having and enjoyed the slow pace for the last few days.

We had two colon cleanses per day, which involved lots of bowel movements to really cleanse the body! It was such an interesting experience and was my first retreat I'd ever done. We ended up going back and doing another one, but more intense. The second time round we fasted for many days. I lasted five days and my friend managed seven. We lived on coconut water and supplements each day. It's amazing what the body can do. We learned so much about nutrition and the power of our bodies when giving the right tools and food. Thailand will always have a special place in my heart and holds so many wonderful memories and where I found another piece of myself to become who I am today.

Do: I invite you to do something adventurous. What would feel daring and exciting for you? Perhaps carve out some time this week orthis month to go do that thing that would feel fun.

Feel: Can you recall a time in your life where you felt energised and refreshed? Where were you and what were you doing?

Think: When you were a child, what did you do that was adventurous and fun?

Journal Prompt: If you were to sprinkle a little more adventure into your life and have more joy and freedom, how would your life change?

MY REFLECTION

9 TAKING RISKS, FLYING SOLO

A REALISATION OF THE RESILIENCE AND BRAVERY I HAVE DEEP WITHIN THROUGH MY SOLO TRAVELS

I'm in the Amazon, South America and feeling all sorts of emotions. Scared. Excited. Out my depth. What am I doing here? I didn't prepare for this trip. What was I thinking?? It's bloody roasting and I didn't bring the right clothes for this weather. I'm here now though so I'll just have to get on with it. It will be okay, think positive...

As I reflect back on the trips I've done solo, there were some situations I found myself in which were sometimes a little scary. Thankfully all was okay, but I share this with you because my advice is that if you are thinking of travelling solo, always have self-awareness, connect to your intuition, and make sure you are safe. Although some things can happen, like what I will share with you, always be mindful and look after yourself. I have grown so much and loved all the travel and adventures, but there were moments where I was like, *Wow, I'm so grateful that turned out okay!*

I was travelling in Peru and part of my trip was to spend three days in the Amazon. From the start of this trip, it really was a disaster. I laugh now looking back, but at the time I was thinking, *Get me out of here!* I'd booked an overnight bus to get from Cusco to the Amazon. All was going well and I fell asleep on the bus peacefully. I then woke around 4am to find we had stopped in the middle of nowhere, still dark. I was confused trying to find out what was going on, but speaking little Spanish certainly made that more challenging. I got into a conversation with a man who was sitting across from me, a local, and he advised that due to a conflict between two small towns, some boulders and rocks had been placed over the road which meant that we couldn't travel any further.

In that moment I had to decide whether to stay and wait to see what will happen, or this man I had been speaking with advised me that he was going to walk to the next town which would take around an hour and then get a car from there to where we wanted to go. I decided to go with this man. We set off and started to walk the road. I felt nervous but something inside of me trusted the man I was with. What didn't help was that I had totally overpacked for this trip and my bag was so heavy, after twenty minutes of walking I was exhausted. It was so hot compared to Cusco, which I also didn't prepare for. You'd think I would check the weather, hey?

I was so disorganised for this trip. Earlier that day, before I'd got the bus, I ended up meeting some lovely people in a bar and we had some drinks together and had so much fun chatting and sharing stories. This meant that when I got back to my home to get ready for this trip, I really didn't think it through, hence the overweight bag.

During my stay in the Amazon, it really was something. I think mentally, after what I'd experienced getting to the Amazon, I didn't fully embrace and enjoy the wonders of it the way I had hoped to. But I still look at it as an experience in its own magical way. I was staying in a wooden hut, like a bungalow style. We had no Wifi and only limited electricity during the day. During the evening I'd use a torch to get me from my hut to the place where we had dinner each evening. I didn't sleep at all during that trip. It felt like the whole place came alive during the night and I literally felt like there were animals, insects, everything inside that hut with me. So I felt like I slept on edge, one eye shut, one eye open.

The next story I am about to share with you, I always smile at as it's one of my mum's favourite ones, in a sense that she literally freaked out when I told her about it but at the same time finds it hilarious thinking about me in that situation and loves to share with others. Our tour guide took us out on a boat trip during the day, and again later that evening. During the day we explored the lake and the tour guide took us to a point where we could go into the lake and be in the water. We also did some

67

walking around the Amazon, where I saw my first tarantula and snake. The noises and smells were incredible; the place really awakened my senses. The air was moist and I felt so sticky in my clothes, but tried my best to just be with the experience and take in each moment.

Later that evening, the tour guide told us that the lake we had been swimming in had piranhas in it. I almost died with shock, *What did you say? Piranhas?!* I thought perhaps he was messing around, but indeed it was true as he showed us that evening by throwing pieces of raw meat into the lake and we could see them snatching it. I couldn't believe I had been in that water only a few hours earlier and shivers chilled down my spine.

During our next adventure in the lake that evening, the tour guide took us out again on the boat to explore the lake under the shining moon. As we slowly moved through the lake, the tour guide began to make some sound, like he was calling something. I was intrigued, wondering what it was, and the next moment I could see something in the water start to move towards us. The closer it got, I realised it was a crocodile. I felt terrified as it came right beside us on the boat. I threw my hoodie over my head and could feel my heart racing. I looked out again and, as I turned to look at the crocodile, it was still and its eyes were on me. It looked so calm but like it could just attack in any moment. At least that's what my mind was telling me. The tour guide was laughing at me and explained that it had been fed so wasn't interested in eating me. We finally ventured back to land and I have never felt so happy to be back in a safe place.

It's funny. Some of the experiences I have been through, had I known in advance what was coming, I'd probably talk myself out of doing such things. In that moment though, you have no option but to just go with it. I think I prefer it that way to be honest. It's good to have lots of interesting stories to tell my future children.

Cusco, Peru.

Wow, I feel so at home here. What is it about this place that is lighting something up inside of me? As I walk up this path, surrounded by beauty, there's a sense of calmness all around me and inside of me. I could live here, I think to myself. I want to spend more time here.

I absolutely loved Peru. It's one of my favourite places I've visited. I felt at home there, like I was connected to the land and the people. It was the first place where I truly experienced hiking and what my body was capable of. Cusco, where I stayed most of my trip, has an altitude of 11,200ft. I was told that I may experience some altitude sickness symptoms during this trip, but thankfully I was okay. I drank the local coco tea which helped. I had a couple of minor headaches and it took a few days for my lungs to adapt to it, so walking up hills I easily got short of breath. I remember being there a couple of days when I went out for dinner and met a lovely man from the US. We ended up hanging out that evening and after a few cocktails, I was so drunk! If you can imagine that feeling you get when you are on a flight and you have a drink and it goes to your head, it was like that.

I visited some beautiful places in Peru. My favourites being Lake Titicaca, Rainbow Mountain and, of course, Macchu Picchu. Some of the hikes I did really tested me, between my mind freaking out with the intensity of them but also this realisation of how incredible and strong my body was. All of them were challenging in their own ways.

Lake Titicaca for example, tested me through a steep climb. I remember looking up thinking, *When will this end?* It felt like a never-ending climb. My heart was beating so fast through my chest. I had to keep having an inner conversation with myself, telling myself that I could do it, that I was strong and capable enough to do it, and to just focus on each step I was taking. When I finally arrived at the lake, it was absolutely breath-taking and so beautiful. I felt so alive and so proud of myself. I felt such gratitude for my body, for that moment.

Rainbow Mountain… Wow, I'm in awe. With an altitude of 17000ft this was another interesting and out my depth challenge. This height is the same as the base camp of Mount Everest and also the height of where you would jump off a plane to do a sky dive. So you can imagine, pretty high. I really had to take my time with this walk, only a few steps and I was out of breath. As I walked I was joined by another man. I remember him trying to talk to me and I said to him I am afraid I can't speak otherwise I won't be able to walk as I felt like I had to keep my energy and my breath to just do the climb. During the climb, I noticed oxygen tanks for people incase they were in need of them. I remember thinking, *What the F?* I could feel my mind beginning to panic, but I told myself it was going to be okay. There were also some donkeys along the way if someone needed assistance getting to the top. Slowly but surely, step by step, I made it. I made it! Ah, once again I was in awe. In awe of my body, of this journey, of this moment. It was absolutely beautiful. It was like a canvas and it didn't feel real. I found a new deep sense of appreciation for my body and what it was doing.

Finally, Macchu Picchu… oh what a wonder you truly are! I was ready to embark on the 4-day trek and fully experience this journey.

I was joined by three Italian guys who made the trip humorous and enjoyable. We camped each night, had a team of locals who would always be in front to prepare our tents and food for us. They were incredible beings! Strong and fast. They amazed me. Every stop along the way, they would be there waiting for us, all set up with lovely homemade food to keep us energised.

Having four days with no internet I thoroughly enjoyed. Just being in the moment, day by day, taking everything in. Thinking about the Incas, those who lived here many years before. What must it have been like to live in those days? I found my mind wandering with imagination.

One day in particular I found really tough. It was a constant climb, for about 7 hours. I felt so exhausted, mentally and physically. The last hour of it I was joined by a man from another expedition company; we chatted a little and he told me of stories from other places he had hiked. I loved his enthusiasm and how his face lit up. I love this in everyone I meet with and when we share travel stories. It's like my soul lights up and I see that mirrored in the other person. I believe before I was born into this world that it was one of my soul's purposes, to grow and expand through travelling.

I really enjoyed the company of the Italians during this trip. During our moments of challenge, of when we felt tired, we would always bring some humour into the moment and I feel we helped each other. They were kind men and would always make sure I was okay.

Each day I was in awe by the views. The smells, the noises around me. My whole body felt alive with it all.

On the final day, we woke at 3am in order to get to the Sun Gate for it opening. The Sun Gate is a beautiful viewpoint over the whole of Macchu Picchu and we went there before entering Macchu Picchu. We had arrived. The last four days had brought us to this point. I didn't want it to end. I wanted to soak up every last minute. We spent some time walking around and the tour guide gave us a lovely exploration of the history of this incredible place. Again I found myself dreaming and imagining all those who lived here and what it must have been like. Once we had explored and left, we got the train back to Cusco, which was also a really enjoyable experience as we all shared a drink and toasted to our experience and shared our stories and highlights.

As I write this, I feel tears come to my eyes with such gratitude of my time in Peru. It really was so special and will always have a place in my heart. I hope to one day visit again and I am sure I will.

Do: I invite you to do something that feels brave. It could be as simple as taking one little step in a particular area of your life. An aligned step towards a goal you may have.

Feel: Where in your life do you feel bravery or resilient? Can you recall a memory that allows you to feel that?

Think: Have you ever been in a situation where you felt out of your comfort zone? What did you experience?

Journal Prompt: If you were to live your life feeling braver and more resilient with what life throws at you, what would your life look and feel like?

MY REFLECTION

DATE   /   /

10   BEHIND THE MASQUE

WHO I AM IS NOT DEFINED BY HOW I LOOK

Hello first day at secondary school. I don't know a single person here. Why did we have to move home?, I wonder to myself. I feel out my depth and so self-conscious with my skin. Trying to fit in to new surroundings and meet new people, but also trying to hide. Little do I know that this will be the beginning of a challenging but also deeply healing experience.

For over a decade I was so consumed with my skin and how I looked. At the tender age of 13 I developed Acne which stayed with me until around the age of 28. Every single day I thought about my skin. I spent years putting on a masque through a lot of makeup and always looking the part in the clothes I wore, hair extensions and normally a set of heels. I'd created this idea in my head from what I'd witnessed growing up, that in order to fit in it was all about how I looked. Having Acne and my face being what people saw first, I felt so seen and vulnerable most of my life.

For a long time I was lost in looks. Lost in perfection, lost in the external. I remember whilst I was dating, I'd wake up earlier to top up my makeup with the fear of the guy seeing me bare faced and not liking what he saw. I would go on holiday and I'd be wearing a full face of makeup whilst sunbathing on the beach. I'd be at after parties following nights in clubs and I'd already be thinking of the morning, with the daylight light almost upon me and thinking, *Is my face okay?* Checking in the toilet mirror if I needed to top it up. I compared myself to friends and other girls at school and be envious of the way they looked, how perfect their skin was and what it must be like to not have that concern.

I had this belief that in order to be loved and be accepted was based on what I looked like. This stayed with me for a long time, even in my mid-twenties whilst living in Saudi. I would be relaxing at the pool with friends during the weekend and I could be in constant thought of my appearance and wondering if they were thinking the same as me, how bad it was. Even writing this feels very vulnerable to share, as this way of being and thinking was with me for a very long time.

I was yet to discover that true beauty lies within; who I am, my values and how I am showing up in the world authentically, is so much more than what I look like.

My skin did start to clear up later in my twenties through medication, which I wouldn't personally recommend but by that point it was a last resort for me. However, during that time, my journey with nutrition was also beginning to unfold and I was starting to take some natural supplements which I believe all helped me to bring my body back to balance. From that, my skin healed, my menstrual cycle regulated and my hormones were more in flow. I can see now how it was all connected.

Fast forward a few years when I returned home from Saudi, I remember the concern around how I looked reappearing. I was working with a coach at the time and I remember saying to her how I'd felt more comfortable and at ease in myself, especially when I was living away and travelling, but something was triggered inside of me again when I was back living in my home town. I believe this was actually my younger self reacting to what I'd lived through and experienced before and she felt scared about being seen. It was like I'd connected to my teenage self again and was re-living those same thoughts and feelings.

I took some time to understand what I was experiencing and stepped out of my comfort zone by travelling to the city bare faced and allowing myself to have days out and about with no makeup on. It sounds crazy but it helped me so much and I was able to give love and acceptance to my younger self by doing this; showing her that it was okay and that I didn't need to be defined by this way of thinking or being anymore.

The relationship I have now with my skin is much more compassionate and loving. I can have days not wearing any makeup which was huge for me. I can be around people barefaced and I don't have the thoughts I used to. I still have the odd breakout but it doesn't effect me the way it used to. I believe this is due to finding more peace in myself and feeling more at home in my body. My skin doesn't define me and neither does appearance. My energy and how I am being each day, the values I hold and the woman I choose to be, with so much compassion and love towards myself, allows me to be okay with all that I am. I am grateful for my flaws and parts of myself that perhaps I had disowned before, as they have made me the woman I am today and to be able to appreciate myself so much more.

Do: I invite you to spend some time looking at yourself in the mirror. Play a song that feels good and, as the song plays, gently look into your own eyes for the whole song. Notice what emotions come up for you, and welcome them in.

Feel: When you think about the relationship you have with yourself, what comes up for you? What feelings and emotions arise for you? Allow yourself to have compassion and love towards whatever is there.

Think: In what ways do you find yourself seeking validation outside of yourself?

Journal Prompt: If true beauty lies within, and you could accept all parts of yourself just as you are in this moment, right here right now, how would your life unfold and what would change?

MY REFLECTION

11   FEELING FREE AND WILD

GIVING MYSELF PERMISSION TO BE WILD AND FREE THROUGH WHAT BRINGS ME JOY

It's 4am and I am dancing like a crazy person in a nightclub in Glasgow. I can't stop, I won't stop. This is it, this is life. I feel high and in love - it can't get any better than this can it? I feel a surge of love moving through my body as I dance to the rhythm. What a feeling.

Throughout my life, I've been a lover of music and dance. You would find me dancing my heart out at a few favourite clubs in Glasgow which then led me to travel to different countries to see some of my favourites DJs. Leaving home at the young age of 17 and moving to the city literally changed my life, as I started to explore the music scene and found myself in awe of this new world I found myself entering into. I think it was the first time I found a sense of freedom and could just be myself. I was a dancer when I was younger, so I always had that step in me and, combined with good music, I'd just let go and have so much fun. Even now when I find myself feeling overwhelmed, or too much in my head, I put on a few of my favourite songs and drop into my body and move. It helps me to feel more centred, in the moment, and brings a sense of calm all over me. Music and movement are definitely a healing modality for me and have been all my life.

One of the most awakening and profound experiences I had was when I went to Burning Man in Nevada. I will never forget the feeling I had when I landed there and explored the playa. It was bliss. It was incredible. It was out of this world. We spent a week there and I had the most amazing time dancing to world class DJs, meeting genuinely lovely people, wearing the craziest and most wild outfits and floating around on my bicycle. I remember my friend saying to me the first day we ventured out and were on our bikes, "The look on your face Sam, it's priceless, I have been waiting for this moment as I knew how much you were going to love it here!"

She had been once before so already had a feel of the place. Ah, even writing this now puts such a big smile on my face.

We lived in an RV and would cook meals for each other, preparing for each day and excited about what was to come. One of the rules of experiencing Burning Man was 'no mans land' which meant once the event was finished, you don't leave a trace behind. Pick up all of your rubbish and things, and off you go. I loved that.

I met so many wonderful people, had many deep conversations and received some beautiful gifts as a token of appreciation from the connection we had. I also gave some gifts when I too felt a deep connection with another person. It was a way of saying thank you, thank you for this moment together to just be. I felt so free, alive and connected during that trip.

Returning to Saudi after the experience of Burning Man, I found myself still in this high vibe state and feeling so relaxed and content with life. Something had changed inside of me. I was waking up naturally and at ease with every day life. I felt so connected and in deep gratitude for the moments I'd had there. This feeling stayed with me for a few weeks following the trip and, looking back, I feel that I'd experienced a sense of total freedom being my authentic self and I wanted more of that.

Do: I invite you to be wild today. Do something that feels free and alive in your entire being.

Feel: Can you remember a time where you felt wild and free? Where were you and what were you doing?

Think: What does wild mean to you?

Journal Prompt: If you could live your life wildly and unapologetically, what would you do more of?

MY REFLECTION

DATE   /   /

12 SOUL CONNECTIONS

THE MORE I AM MY TRUE AUTHENTIC SELF, THE MORE I ATTRACT MY SOUL TRIBE

Here I am. Tender age of 17 and feeling confused within friendships. It just doesn't feel good. I feel like I don't fit in. Is it me? I decide to walk away. I go home and I tell my mum I can't do it another day. I feel alone. But in this moment when I look back, I will realise what a huge step I have made towards finding my soul tribe.

Throughout my life, I've had challenges with connection but also had some of the most wonderful connections with others. I feel I deeply crave connection, a sense of belonging, however, I do recognise times in my life where I've also not let people in. Where I isolated myself and had moments of wanting to be alone because I felt that was a safer option. I believe that this all came from fear of rejection or abandonment.

Growing up I had experiences of rejection from others, whether it be from a boy I liked at school or through a friendship where a friend wasn't there for me as much as I wanted them to be. So, I guess I formed the belief that maybe it was better to just do it alone because that way I wouldn't get hurt. Yet, what I found was that through believing these thoughts and beliefs, I ended up rejecting myself throughout my life which then attracted people in my life who mirrored this to me, like a confirmation of this 'truth' I had ingrained to myself. However, I also do recognise times in my life where I've walked away from environments and situations in my life where I felt that I deserved more.

My first experience of this was when I was around 17. I was part of a large group of friends and we partied most weekends. It was an interesting experience, as all throughout my teenage years I deeply craved to be part of a 'popular' crowd and then suddenly I found myself in it and I had never felt so alone. I remember the girls at the time complimenting each other on their outfits but they would never compliment me. I felt like an outsider and found myself going more inward and feeling like I didn't have a voice to share. I felt like I didn't fit in and questioned whether being in this crowd was actually worthwhile or if I should walk away from it. After months of spending time with them, I remember going home to my mum one day and I burst into tears and told her how I felt. I just felt so alone and didn't feel that I could be a part of it anymore. That day I decided to walk away. It was one of the hardest things I did because I suddenly found myself with no friends at all.

Looking back, I see that this was a pivotal point of my life which actually geared me into a new and exciting direction of my life. It was at this point I decided to move out of my family home and took the leap to move to the city. From this space and having no attachments, it felt like I could start again. Over the years I began to make new friends, genuine connections. People I felt that I could be myself with and be vulnerable with. I formed new friendships through my clubbing days and also formed some from workplaces.

Moving to Saudi I found my Saudi family too, who are still some of my closest friends. Friends that I can laugh with and cry with, friends that I can open my heart with and tell them my darkest secrets. Friends who I can call on and know that they have my back. Friends who I've been on the most wonderful adventures with and shared so many beautiful memories with.

Even over the last couple of years, I feel my connections have grown even more. I feel this has come from the work I've done on myself; the more I've grown to love appreciate myself and my uniqueness, the more I've attracted soul connections. I feel my experiences of being held in women's circles has also helped with this and I began to gain trust again in other women. I always leave them feeling so deeply connected, with my heart wide open and a sense of belonging.

Do: Reach out to a someone who you feel is a member of your soul tribe and tell them how much you appreciate and love them.

Feel: What does a true and authentic friendship feel like for you?

Think: If you were surrounded by people who support you and celebrate you, how would this impact your life?

Journal Prompt: Recall a memory where you were with someone you love dearly and had the most amazing time together. Write down what you experienced and why you are so grateful for that experience.

MY REFLECTION

DATE   /   /

13 THE HIGHS AND LOWS OF DATING

REALISING THAT ACCEPTANCE AND LOVE OF
SELF COMES FROM WITHIN AND THAT
ANYTHING OUTSIDE OF THAT IS JUST AN
EXTENSION OF THE LOVE I ALREADY HAVE FOR
MYSELF

My my, the dating world. Once again I'm home after a date with a guy and it hasn't turned out the way I'd hoped. He didn't call me back. He doesn't want to meet up again. I find myself meeting guys I like but it's just not going the way I want it to. What's wrong with me? Is it me? Or maybe it's him. I'm better than this! Oh, but I just want to find love. Help.

I feel that my dating experiences have been a big part of my life. I guess because it's something that I've desired all my life, to meet someone that I have a romantic and deep connection with. A soul mate, twin flame, lover, best friend. Throughout my whole life I've been in one serious relationship, which lasted almost 2 years. So I have been 'alone' or whatever you would call it, for most of my life.

There were many dates, a few one night stands and a couple more casual relationships. I would lose myself in men. I desperately wanted to meet someone I could be with for the rest of my life. I had this belief that in order to be happy, it would be through meeting someone and spending the rest of my days with them. Well, this has certainly been a test for me throughout my life and maybe it's one of my soul lessons for this lifetime, who knows.

My first love was when I was 17. I was head over heels. I guess it was the first time I felt such lust and connection with someone. However, it was also the first time I experienced a guy who was emotionally unavailable and played with my feelings again and again, because I let him. We would date for a bit, then it would stop, then he would go back with his ex, and then all over again. This went on for about 2 years until eventually we decided no more and moved on. It was the first time I felt heartbroken - I really cared for him and wanted to be with him, but he didn't feel the same way. It left me feeling confused, this dance between letting me in and pushing me away. After this experience, it was probably the first time I closed off my heart, with the fear of letting that happen again.

Fast forward a few years and I found myself dating many guys, and was always attracting men who wanted nothing more than sex. Most of them were emotionally unavailable and didn't want what I wanted. I wanted someone to want me and not just for one night. *Why was it that I kept attracting this type of man?* For many years I really didn't know and just kept going for that same type of energy and would always be left feeling unwanted, that I wasn't enough and wondering was I ever going to meet someone.

I entered my first relationship in my early twenties and remembered feeling so excited that it was developing into something more serious. I felt that we had a nice connection, shared some lovely experiences together and I enjoyed my time with him. However, after a year or so I noticed a change in him, he seemed distant and wasn't in touch with me as much as he had been before. I started to feel anxious and that same feeling I'd had with men before was coming up for me again. I ended up turning up at his house one day to talk to him and find out what was going on. That day also ended the relationship as, after having a conversation with him and being honest with how I was feeling, he wasn't prepared to put in the effort and meet me where I was at. Not long after we split, I found out that he had gone back to his ex. Perhaps it was going on when we were still together and that would explain the distance I felt with him, but I'll never know.

As I reflect and think about my life and dating, I've definitely looked to find happiness and fulfilment in meeting someone. I believed that would be it. Once I met him everything would all work out. I now know this isn't true and that true peace and happiness must come from myself and the relationship I have with myself. Any man who comes into my life is just an extension of the life I've already created for myself. Of course, it will be wonderful to create a life with someone but it's important for me to be mindful of not losing myself in it. To have healthy boundaries in place and know that it's my responsibility to deal with challenges that may come up in my life. To communicate clearly what I want from the relationship and have an openness to it. To listen deeply to my partner and build a solid foundation with each other from the start. I also recognise that the reason I was attracting someone who was emotionally unavailable was because deep down I didn't feel worthy of love and I didn't feel enough. I was attracting men that mirrored that. I also feel that it was a way of protecting myself because I was so scared of being hurt again. I felt fear of showing parts of myself that I already disliked and being rejected, as I was already rejecting myself.

Have I met my man yet? No. But I believe I will, and perhaps there's a few more tests for me to go through yet. I'm okay with that. The most important thing I've been learning through this journey is the relationship I have with myself and to not run away from myself. To love all parts of myself and that I am enough. That I am worthy and deserving of love and to find someone that mirrors that.

Of course, there will still be challenges and I believe when I move into a relationship with someone, it will be a great opportunity to see what else has been hiding and what else I need to face within myself. Finally, I also see that I don't need someone else to make me happy. It is my responsibility to make my life more joyous, loving and free and, when I meet that person, he will just be an extension of an already deeply fulfilled life.

THE HIGHS AND LOWS OF DATING - PRESCRIPTION

Do: Spend some time with yourself filling yourself up with love, doing things that feel so good and nourishing for your mind, body and soul. You are worth it.

Feel: What does a healthy romantic relationship look like for you? What qualities would the relationship have and how would you like to feel?

Think: What has your journey so far been like within romantic relationships and what have you learned?

Journal Prompt: If you loved up on you and filled up your own cup before giving yourself to others, how would this feel? How would your life change?

MY REFLECTION

DATE   /   /

14 MAKING DIFFICULT CHOICES
SOMETIMES IN LIFE I HAVE TO MAKE DIFFICULT BUT NECESSARY CHOICES

It's a Sunday afternoon and I am feeling a bit off. I've heard this whisper saying 'Take a test to make sure'. After texting my friend, I decide to go to the shop I buy two pregnancy tests just to rule it out... almost certain that I am not pregnant. Shit, I am. In a flash my whole world is turned upside down.

When I was moving through my journey with a hormonal imbalance, I didn't bleed for over a year when I came off The Pill. During this time, I was also dating a guy that I'd met whilst living in Saudi. Having a non-existent bleed, I thought it would have been impossible for me to fall pregnant; by having no bleed, essentially, I wasn't ovulating. Or at least that was what I believed. We were always careful having sex, but after one of our weekends together, something in me kept urging me to take a pregnancy test. I kept putting it off as I genuinely thought there was way that I'd conceived. However, this urge got the better of me and a few weeks later I decided to take a test just to make sure. I remember speaking to my friend that day and us having a conversation about it and we both agreed that I was probably just over thinking it. However, that day my life was changed in an instant. I was pregnant and in so much shock. I couldn't believe it. I took another test just to clarify it, and again it was positive. So many thoughts were running around in my head and I felt overwhelmed about what to do. I wasn't even with the guy I had been dating, as I'd decided to call it off as I wasn't feeling it with him. I went to the hospital the following day and had a scan to confirm that I was around 6 weeks pregnant. The lady who was my nurse congratulated me and I burst into tears. I wasn't ready to have a child and if I went through with the pregnancy, I'd have lost my job in Saudi and would have to moved home.

The next day I spoke to my family and had to make one of the most difficult choices I'd made in my life, to have an abortion. It was even more challenging because I was living in a country where it was illegal, so I couldn't tell anyone the truth of what I was going through (apart from my closest friends). So, within that week I had to book a flight home, make some excuse to take time off work and go home to have the procedure. The days that followed were a blur. I went into some kind of operational mode, getting myself home, booking what needed to be done and moving through the whole process. I felt that the decision was the right one for me at that time of my life but I also felt an overwhelming sadness as I did want to and still do want to have children, but I couldn't have at that stage of my life. My life would have taken a completely different path and I was happy with the life I had living abroad, having no responsibilities and just looking after myself. I didn't feel at all ready.

The experience itself felt like loss, just like grief. I can understand that more fully now, but at the time I probably didn't as much. I remember returning to my sister's home after being at the hospital, feeling absolutely exhausted, and I ended up having a panic attack. I think it was from the build up of everything I was going through and my body went into a huge adrenaline release. I had to return back to Saudi a few days following the procedure and went back into my day to day life.

A few months later, it hit me hard. I found myself isolated and feeling really overwhelmed. Something wasn't right. I was crying a lot and felt a deep sadness in me. At first I didn't connect it with the abortion, but then I started doing some journaling and found I was writing about my experience and what I'd gone through. I ended up reaching out to someone I'd found online and did some therapy sessions with them to help me process what I'd gone through. Over time, I felt more at ease and was able to be with everything that happened and the decision I'd made, even through it was truly one of the most challenging ones I had to make. I hope one day I will have children, as I really would love to be a mother and experience everything that comes with motherhood.

MAKING DIFFICULT CHOICES - PRESCRIPTION

Do: If you have experienced some form of loss that felt difficult, if it feels comfortable for you, I invite you to spend some time reflecting on your experience and journal on what you went through. Writing can be such a beautiful and healing way of releasing the experience on to paper, whilst welcoming any emotions that may arise.

Feel: How do you feel when you have to make difficult but necessary choices? Is it something you find easy or uncomfortable?

Think: Can you recall a time in your life when you had to make a choice that was difficult but you came through the other side? What happened?

Journal Prompt: I invite you to spend some time to reflect and journal on times in your life where you had to make difficult but necessary choices. Through this, also reflect on what attributes about yourself that helped you make those choices (for example, one for me was resilience).

MY REFLECTION

15 SEEKING LOVE AND VALIDATION OUTSIDE OF MYSELF

REALISING THAT I AM ALREADY WHOLE AND ENOUGH JUST AS I AM

It suddenly lands, deeply. What if all I am searching for what I already am? What if I am already enough and there is nothing to change? How would that feel, I ask myself. And suddenly there is a moment of openness and a calm feeling washes over me. I don't have to do anything, I am already that. It begins to feel like a weight has been lifted off my shoulders and I can breathe again.

Throughout my life, I deeply searched for love outside of myself. I deeply searched for validation from others that I was good enough. I looked for it in men, from friendships, work colleagues and family. I so wanted to fit in and feel loved and accepted by others. I'd find myself saying yes to things when I really didn't want to; I was a people pleaser and felt afraid to speak my truth or to share what I wanted. I'd put people on a pedestal and look up to them like they were more than me and see things in others that I wanted to be, as if telling myself that I lacked something. And even if people did say that they loved me, or complimented me or even celebrated me, it never felt enough. I was always seeking and yearning for more. It was like I could hear the words they were saying but I didn't accept it or allow myself to fully receive it.

I can now see where this all stemmed from, and I know a lot of it came from my younger years at school and when my skin started to breakout. I received hurtful comments and started to believe that how I looked wasn't good enough, or pretty enough. From a very young age I was already comparing myself to others and felt that who I was 'externally' wasn't accepted by the cultural norm I was experiencing. Through this journey I got lost in my external appearance and didn't value who I was as a being and all I had to share with the world, like my uniqueness, gifts or talents.

With men, I'd find myself doing what they wanted to do, rather than asking myself what I wanted. Within friendships I'd allow others to take control and agree to what they wanted, rather than check in with myself and see if it felt right for me. Within work I'd experience managerial staff who would speak unkindly to me, and I felt afraid to share my truth or express that I wasn't comfortable with the way I was being treated. Within my family, I'd just accept what was and be the quiet girl, not wanting to upset anyone or cause any more conflict in certain situations. I had shut down my power. I had disowned my voice and felt afraid to speak up. I guess I felt that, in order to be safe, was to be unseen and unheard.

When I started to unravel these patterns, beliefs and stories I had about myself, I realised that in order to feel loved, validated and accepted, it had to come from me. No one else could give that to me. That's why, when someone else gave me a compliment or said something nice to me, it never felt enough. I'd instantly reject it because I didn't believe it was true. I started to realise that by people pleasing or saying yes to things I didn't want to, I was hurting myself more and I was giving away my power.

Over time, I have been unlearning what I believed to be true and creating a new story. I have been collecting new evidence to show myself that I am enough and that it is about who I am being, and the energy that I desire to be. That all I am seeking I can give to myself, in a very loving and compassionate way. I have spent time with my inner child, nourishing her and giving her space to speak, to speak of what she was afraid to before. I have danced with it, moved through it and given myself space to be with everything I am. I have faced the shadow sides of myself, the parts I'd disowned and the parts I didn't like.

I started saying no to things that didn't feel right and leaning more about what does. I found that I started to attract more meaningful relationships and environments that mirrored where I was at. It was like the more I attended to and started to change my inner world, my outer world reflected this change and for the better.

Don't get me wrong, this is an ongoing journey and I still face challenges. Things still come my way to test me and it can feel uncomfortable at times. But, deep down, I know that the more I keep coming back home to myself and trusting myself, and the more I embody all that I am, the more I will feel enough just as I am.

Do: Take some time out today, even just 5 minutes, and be in a seated position. Place your hands on your heart and breathe into your heart space. Imagine your heart is opening. As you breathe in, say internally to yourself, "I am love", and as you breathe out say, "I am whole."

Feel: You are already enough just as you are. Really, you are! How does that feel? Can you allow yourself to lean into that more?

Think: What stories do you have around needing to receive validation or approval outside of yourself? Where do you think this has come from?

Journal Prompt: Imagine you are content with all parts of yourself, just as you are. All of you is welcome. You're smiling and feeling good about yourself. Write down what you are experiencing in your life as you step into this energy.

MY REFLECTION

DATE   /   /

16 MAKING FRIENDS WITH SALLY, AKA THE 'EGO'

MY EGO WILL ALWAYS TRY TO KEEP ME SAFE AND PROTECT ME, BUT I CHOOSE TO LIVE AND LEAD FROM MY HEART MORE OFTEN

Hello Sally, aka ego. Yes, I hear you. I know you just want to keep me safe once again, and I appreciate that. But I'm okay and I know what I'm doing, my heart is yearning for this. I know it's a little scary but I can do this. I am going to do this.

———

Throughout my life, I've often allowed my mind to run the show. Over analysing vs. over thinking. Fear and anxiety creeping up for me from the thoughts I find myself consuming and believing. Sometimes the voice felt so loud I felt like I wanted to scream and run away from myself. I've had moments where my mind just goes blank and nothing is there, like I've completely forgot how to think. I'd find myself wondering if it's because my mind in overdrive and is literally exhausted from thinking.

Over-thinking had an impact on various areas of my life, like the food I'd consume which would lead to overeating or cancelling on friends and family as I'd talk myself out of it and isolate myself. Even within my business, the fear of stepping into some events that I'd organised, it would consume me so much I'd be on the verge of having a panic attack and would cancel everything. I believe it's also what caused panic attacks; so much overdrive and so many thoughts running around in my head without giving myself space to share how I was feeling or what I was experiencing. It was as if my body went into overdrive which then led on to a panic attack.

I also felt I had to be in control of my life and know the outcome of most things as a way of feeling safe and I feel a lot of that was coming from my mind. Having a certain routine and structure and having things a certain way helped me feel more in control of my external world.

Over time, I've developed a love-hate relationship with my mind, or another word you could use is the 'ego'. I understand that she's just trying to protect me and keep me safe, but sometimes it made me feel so small and useless when I am over consumed with the thoughts and patterns that repeat in my head. I'd decided to call her Sally and try and make friends with her. It's not always been easy, but in other ways it's helped me to detach from the stories that may come up for me, the limited beliefs, and to self-inquire into those thoughts and patterns and really question, I*s this actually true? Where did this thought, or* *belief come from?* From this space, I would have more clarity and ease, and with the awareness and understanding of where it may have come from, start to have more compassion and love towards myself and the patterns I'd formed.

I also feel that in those times when my mind and thoughts had taken over, I felt less disconnected to my intuition and to my truth. It was driven by fear, a fear of being left out, rejected, or even deeper… abandonment. I made irrational decisions and did things that I didn't want to do. I'd find myself in situations where I'd say yes but really, I wanted to say no. There were times where I trusted my mind over my heart, but it led me to feeling empty, unfulfilled and somewhat shame around my decisions.

Over time it's been a slow and gentle process of having awareness of my thoughts and, when making decisions, to connect with my heart and body more often, allowing myself time to sit with the invitation before saying yes or no. Feeling at one with my body and seeing if I get a good feeling about it, or not, so it's more of a body based yes or no.

A greater realisation I found from all of this, was that it was okay to say no and that I didn't have to even give a reason as to why I was saying no. This was huge for me, because even the times I used to say no or cancel, I would find myself wanting to justify my reasons through the fear of that person feeling hurt or not wanting to spend any more time with me, or even simply to avoid confrontation.

Through this work, it also led me to look at boundaries within my life and begin to say yes to the things that felt in alignment and saying no to those that did not.

I also have had to accept that my mind will always try to run the show and, in order to not get caught up with it, it's about me being more present in each moment and in each day. Connecting to my breath really helps with this; even just taking a few deep breaths brings me back into my body and into the moment and reminds me that I am okay and that I am safe.

Another tool that helps me is dropping into my body through movement, I'll put on some music I love and start to move my body in an embodied way and also take some deep breaths. Through this process, it helps me feel more anchored and at ease and is another reminder to myself that I am safe I tell my mind, "I hear you, thank you for doing your best to protect me, but I got this."

Do: The next time you find your mind trying to protect you and keep you safe, notice what is coming up for you and, if you know in your heart what is good for you, gently whisper to your self, "I hear you and thank you, I got this and all is well."

Feel: Do you feel consumed by your thoughts sometimes? How does it make you feel?

Think: If you could connect more to your heart and make decisions from there, what would change?

Journal Prompt: Imagine your life is more balanced and at ease as you are starting to make more heartfelt decisions and you are more aware of your ego. How is your life unfolding?

MY REFLECTION

DATE   /   /

17 EXPRESSING AND WELCOMING ALL EMOTIONS

THE MORE I WELCOME ALL MY EMOTIONS, THE MORE I LIVE A MORE ENRICHED AND FULL LIFE

I am feeling so much frustration right now. Frustration that I sometimes get in my own way and, in doing so, I block myself from experiencing a more fulfilled life that lights me up. I feel you emotion, I welcome you in. I thank you for showing me what's alive in me in this moment. I take a deep breath and breathe into this experience, into my body, and as I do so, I feel the energy begin to move, and it passes.

Being comfortable expressing all of my emotions wasn't always an easy journey. For many years I struggled with expressing anger and speaking my truth. I didn't know how to. Growing up I wasn't taught that expressing and feeling all emotions was normal and actually healthy. As young children we naturally do it. Think of a baby that cries and a toddler that takes a tantrum, it's a way of them expressing how they feel and they do so in a way without caring what anyone around them thinks. Then as we grow up, in some cases, we are conditioned to believe that it's not okay to be loud, to be angry, to be sad. "Be a good girl, be quiet and be seen but not heard" are all things that come to mind when I reflect on my younger years. No disrespect to my parents, they just taught me what they were taught, and didn't know any different.

However, the problems and challenges I faced living this way, and what I learned later in life, was that when I suppressed 'bad' emotions, I also suppressed 'good' emotions. Even labelling them good and bad was giving myself permission to only feel certain ones.

It wasn't until I started doing inner work, and through coaching and mentoring, that I was given the space to express these emotions and in time it felt really good. I remember the first time I was asked to connect with anger and to scream and shout, punch into a pillow and allow myself to really feel it. Initially I found myself laughing at the thought of it and it took me time to really allow myself to feel it. Once I did, I felt empowered, like something inside of me lit up. It was teaching me to express my emotions in a healthy way and by doing so I was opening up myself to feeling the high vibrational emotions like love, joy and pleasure.

I discovered that when I was supressing particular emotions, it would also affect me feeling other emotions like joy etc. I went through most of my life somewhat numb. I would have small peaks of joy and excitement but I was yet to discover that I could actually feel so much more.

My journey with grief after losing my father suddenly amplified this even more. Allowing myself to sit with and be with grief, sadness and pain. It's not always easy and there's times where I feel my heart is so heavy. I question if this will ever go away, but the more I can welcome it and feel it, the more I welcome in love. My journey with grief also showed me other areas of my life where I'd pushed down my feelings through other types of loss, and by doing so my body was consumed with stuck energy, which essentially means I wasn't in my natural flow state.

Each day I do my best to welcome and feel all of my emotions with love. Sometimes it's easy and other times it's still a challenge, but I am human and unlearning years of conditioning and patterns takes time. Another thing that helps is when I feel some emotions, is to self-inquire into what may have brought on this emotion, *is there some tension behind it?* And I can often soften into it from a place of compassion and ease, rather than resisting it and wanting to push it down again. Or, perhaps, when I get triggered by someone or something which is said or done, I ask myself, *why do I feel triggered by this?* It's an invitation for me to go a little deeper and see what unfolds.

I've realised that the more I welcome emotions with ease, the quicker they pass. Emotions are essentially energy - energy that's in motion and is looking for completion. By doing this, I can be more in a flow state, which feels more relaxed rather than a resistant and stuck way of being. Our natural state is flow.

Do: The next time you feel an emotion that you usually want to run away from, I invite you to gently become aware of it and see if you can breathe into it, even if it's just for one minute. Notice if the feeling begins to change and notice how your body feels as you allow yourself to soften into it remembering that an emotion is just energy in motion and that it's okay to feel what you are feeling.

Feel: What emotions do you find challenging to feel? What emotions come easily for you?

Think: Can you remember a time where you felt a strong emotion but then didn't allow yourself to express it? Why did you find it hard to express?

Journal Prompt: If you could allow yourself to open up and feel all emotions, and from that space feel more joy, pleasure and freedom, what areas of your life would change?

MY REFLECTION

DATE   /   /

18 OPENING MYSELF UP TO RECEIVE LOVE

THE MORE I OPEN UP MY HEART, THE MORE I AM OPEN TO LOVE

Mother Ayahuasca. Thank you for showing me how to open myself up to love without necessarily needing your medicine. I am feeling humbled by this experience right now in Portugal with my friends as they help provide a loving and kind space for me as I journey through COVID. I am allowing myself to welcome it all in, to welcome in love.

Life always surprises me. I am always in awe by its twists and turns. Sometimes I resist it and other times I just let it flow. What I've realised is that the more I can just surrender to it and trust that I am always being guided and that life is for me, the more I can be in a state of flow and ease.

A recent experience in my life really showed me the value of just letting it be. I travelled to Lisbon to meet some friends to go on a journey with Ayahuasca. Ayahuasca is a plant medicine and is something I'd been curious of trying over the last few years. After my dad passed away, I felt even more drawn to it, in the hope that I could connect with him on a deeper level and I also wanted to connect more deeply within and open myself up fully to love.

However, what I discovered when I got to the retreat, was that it wasn't the right time for me to journey with Mother Aya. She had other plans. After I arrived, we discovered that the ceremony had to be cancelled due to unforeseen circumstances. Interestingly, a few of us had this instinctual feeling that perhaps the ceremony wasn't going to happen, but we made the plan to go anyway as everything had been arranged. And so with latest news we had received, we adapted and made some changes to the weekend plans.

Two days later after arriving, I came down with COVID which left me feeling physically exhausted and with a fever one evening. In that moment, I knew that one of the reasons why the ceremony didn't happen was because I wouldn't have been physically well for it. I was reminded that, even when I can feel disappointed when something I'd hoped to do doesn't happen, life is actually looking out for me and protecting me.

What was even more interesting was the intention that I'd set myself, which was around me opening myself fully to receiving love, and I sure did receive that. I found myself being nurtured by the others in the group, some of whom I'd never even met before. Being cooked for and looked after. Checking in regularly with me to see if I was okay and if I needed anything. It felt so lovely. I was being shown the kindness, compassion and love of others, and I felt so safe in this space, especially being unwell and away from home.

Another thing that I'd put in my intention was to reconnect with life again fully and appreciate all her beauty, and in this space I was surrounded by beauty, in a gorgeous house in nature, listening to the birds, feeling the wind against my face, the warm sun on my skin and just feeling so deeply connected to Mother Earth again. I feel that because I was physically unwell and having to slow down and rest, I could feel this all more deeply than if had I not been unwell.

The experience also left me feeling deeply connected to others again. I was inspired through conversations and I felt so deeply held and seen. I just felt so much love and, more than anything, it reminded me that I am always being looked after. Life is always for me and the more I can open to that, the more I can just be with life and all it brings my way.

I also trust that I will journey with Mother Aya one day, and that day will come when it's right for me, all in divine timing.

OPENING MYSELF UP TO RECEIVE LOVE - PRESCRIPTION

Do: I invite you to massage your lovely heart. Gently place your left hand onto your chest where your heart is and start massaging your heart in circular motions. This is a wonderful and simple practice to connect to your heart and open yourself up to love.

Feel: Can you remember a time where someone did something kind and loving for you? How did you feel?

Think: Do you find it easy to receive love? Reflect on your answer either way.

Journal Prompt: If you were to fully open yourself up to love, give more love and receive more love, how would your life change from how it is now?

MY REFLECTION   DATE   /   /

19 STEPPING OUT THE COMFORT BUBBLE

LEARNING TO TRUST MY INTUITION, ESPECIALLY IN THE MOST UNCOMFORTABLE MOMENTS

It's 4am and I am leaving my house to travel to the airport. I feel sick and nervous. I never feel like this when I travel. Something feels off. Maybe it's because I've been in a little bubble for quite some time now at home and I am stepping out of it and travelling to another country. Maybe I'm not ready. I want to go back home but something is also pulling me to leave.

I didn't realise how much I was in the comfort bubble, until I stepped out of it. On my latest travels to Portugal, as I packed my things and travelled to the airport, I suddenly felt so raw and out my depth. To be honest, I'd never felt this way when travelling. I always felt so excited and eager for the trip ahead. But this was different. I felt vulnerable and found myself questioning if I had done the right thing. It was as if I had been carrying some emotional baggage without even realising it and, when I stepped away from my comfort zone, my home and my family, it suddenly opened up.

I found myself thinking maybe it was too soon to be travelling alone. Maybe I wasn't ready. It felt too much. But in that, there was also something telling me that I would be okay and that it was something I needed to do. Like there would be a first for everything since my dad's passing.

When I travelled to Lisbon the year following his death, to collect the rest of my stuff, I thought I had passed all the emotions which were coming up for me. Instead what I realised, was that as I'd gone away from my mum and I felt her struggles. I didn't truly feel what was coming up for me because I wanted to make sure my mum was okay. So this experience was surprising to me but, once again, I just had to trust I would be okay and go with it.

On the plane I couldn't stop crying; the tears just kept coming and it was like I was having a huge release. I kept thinking of my dad and felt the depth of how much I missed him and how much my heart yearned to connect with him. That whole day I just cried and cried, allowing myself to feel it all. It was deep. I realised that I had been in a little bubble of safety at home, with my family, day in and day out. By going to Portugal on my own, I was truly given the space to feel it even more; the grief, the pain, the sadness and, of course, deep love for him.

Going back to Portugal alone, the place where I found out about my dad's passing, just brought everything to the surface. I had to fully let it in and surrender to all I was feeling. I visited a couple of places where I felt connected to my dad and allowed myself to be there, immerse in those feelings all over again and to welcome all the emotions in. By doing so, when I returned from this trip, I felt more at peace. I had come to an acceptance with another part of my journey with grief.

I also learned from this experience the closeness I have with my family. I felt such deep gratitude for my mum and my sisters and the bond that we share. Before, I often just took it for granted and would even find myself getting annoyed or frustrated around them and wanting my own space. What I've come to realise is that my family are so supportive and loving and they are just doing their best too. I found myself smiling at how easy going they have been through all my experiences and journeys - they have never judged me or tried to stop me doing the things I've done, even if it perhaps it sounded a little crazy to them. They let me get on with it and I feel so lucky to have that in my life.

STEPPING OUT THE COMFORT BUBBLE - PRESCRIPTION

Do: I invite you to spend some time getting to know the difference between your mind talking vs. your intuition. The mind chatter is usually quite loud, whereas your intuition is softer and feels good, like a deep inner knowing. As you make any decisions, notice if it feels good, like it's coming from your intuition. This is a great way to start trusting yourself more and your inner wisdom.

Feel: Have you ever made a decision that felt so good? Reflect on that memory.

Think: Do you feel connected to your intuition and do you find it easy to make decisions from that place? If not, why do you think that is?

Journal Prompt: Imagine you are living your life fully from your heart and always connected to your intuition - you find it easy to make decisions and know what is good for you. Write down all you are experiencing in a day like this.

MY REFLECTION   DATE   /   /

20 FINDING JOY

LIFE IS SIMPLE AND THE MORE I SLOW DOWN, THE MORE I FEEL GRATITUDE IN THE SMALLEST OF THINGS

I'm seated in a lovely little house in Portugal when I notice a tiny mouse in the kitchen. I'm in awe and my heart melts as I watch him do his thing. I suddenly feel this deep appreciation for witnessing this moment and am reminded of the simplicity of life when I slow down and watch it unfold in front of me.

I am always very curious of the spiritual meaning of animals, so I searched online 'mouse' to see what came up. What I received back really lit something up inside of me. The beauty of small things vs. big things. The appreciation of the tiny little things in life; like a sunrise or sunset, the breath I take so naturally, being able to write this book, being able to see and hear, enjoying a cuppa, eating delicious food, reading a book and connecting with others. Also the freedom I have in day to day life.

I realised how often I can be so consumed with the outcome, that I miss the journey in between. That sometimes when I am in my head too much, I miss the little loving signs along the way. Finding joy in the small things, like waking up and starting a new day, every day, on this beautiful earth. I noticed how often I perhaps don't allow myself the time to really experience joy. There's always a thought of, *What's next?* which essentially disconnects me from the now.

This little mouse reminded me the importance of bringing more joy into my life by appreciating the tiny little things, and not to get lost in the bigger picture. I was reminded to laugh more, to connect more, to appreciate more and to love more. To do my best and be so grateful for each and every day. Joy isn't all the material stuff, it really is the feeling. A feeling of joy inside of me, like dancing and moving my body to music that I love. Or singing to my heart's content. That's all it takes. It can be so simple but sometimes I can too often complicate it.

Joy has now become one of my values in life. I now remind myself to connect with it more often and with ease, like a childlike way of being, and see this humanness on earth like living on an enormous playground.

Sometimes I find it easy, but other times I do still struggle with it. What does help me when I really want to tap into a state of joy, is to think of my younger self and what I was like as a child; care free and not caring about anything but the now. It seems to bring me back into that state of being and puts a smile on my face. My younger self wouldn't be reflecting on the past or worrying about the future, she would be in such awe of the now. It's been a great way to help me connect with her more often too.

Joy can be a natural state, in any moment, if we choose to let it be and I do my best to remind myself of this. Remembering that cute little mouse, so tiny but with so much wisdom to share with me and reminding me of the beauty of life.

Do: Take some time today to slow right down. Notice your surroundings. What do you see? What do you hear? What do you smell? What can you taste?

Feel: Do you find it easy to slow down in life? How does it feel when you do?

Think: If you could live a simplistic life, what three things would make it special?

Journal Prompt: Recall a memory when you were so present in the moment, experiencing joy, and like time had stopped. Journal on your experience.

MY REFLECTION

DATE   /   /

21 LETTING GO OF DOING LIFE ALONE
LIFE IS SO MUCH BETTER WHEN I LET GO OF DOING IT ALL ALONE AND WELCOME IN OTHERS

I'm sitting in circle with a group of women drinking cacao and singing. Suddenly I feel tears streaming from my eyes and I begin to cry. There's a silence within the room but, in that moment, I can feel the women around me as I cry and let go. I feel at home. I feel my body relax and soften and suddenly I am reminded that I don't need to do life alone, that life is so much more loving and fulfilling when doing it together.

For a long time I felt I was better doing things by myself, rather than letting others in to help. From a very young age I became independent and felt that I was better meeting my own needs than letting others support me on my journey. I noticed it in life's day to day events and, even when I moved into my business and received offerings from those around me, I always felt that I had to do everything on my own.

I found it challenging to let support come in. I guess I struggled with trust and believing that I didn't have to do it alone. I've found myself wanting to explore more about this feeling that I had experienced for many years, and consider why it was there. *What would it feel like to let in support, to do it together, rather than on my own?* I've been leaning into this more and what I've realised is that when I allow myself to welcome in support, to be heard and seen or to feel held, it feels really good. It feels like I can soften and relax and that I am part of something so much bigger than doing it on my own. I feel like I come home and I belong.

Where this really came to life for me was during a retreat I attended with a group of 12 women. I've attended many retreats and been a part of many circles where we share, connect, and inspire each other. However, during this particular weekend I felt it really landed in my body. The feeling of being so loved and seen by other women. A celebration of each other and of our highs and lows. The journey we have been on individually, but also collectively. I suddenly felt this deep desire to collaborate with others through my work and wanting to allow support in. It felt really good; the thought of coming together, celebrating each other, sharing our unique gifts and talents, and learning from each other.

I realised that I don't need to do it alone anymore and, actually, I have so much more inspiration and guidance when I connect with other women. It's like all the energy we have within us and around us amplifies and we are connected to something bigger than us, to limitless abundance and potential. When I listened to the other women and their visions, stories and journeys, I felt so much inspiration and wanted to share more of my journey and help them on theirs.

Since this experience, I'm noticing the changes. I've been meeting more friends regularly at home who want to support me and it's felt really nice welcoming it in. It's funny actually, because as I write this, I am sitting in a yurt - I've decided to take myself away for a couple of days alone - but in fact, inside I am thinking, *Where are the others?* I smile as I say that because it's really nice to notice that I am letting more people in, and I want to experience more with others than I've ever felt before.

Of course, I still love a bit down time and my little rituals alone, but I want more fun, more joy and more experiences with others too. I guess at a primal level, when I think about it, we were born in tribe, gathering together, supporting one another. So maybe that's deep within me and now it's yearning to come out and for me to bring that love and support in and that it is okay to do so. I really don't need to do life alone.

Do: I invite you to organise something with a friend/friends/family. Bring a few of you together and do something that would make your heart sing. Allow yourself to receive love from others and have fun together, bringing in connection.

Feel: Reflect on a memory where you felt connection with others. What were you doing and how did it feel?

Think: Do you prefer to do things alone or with others?

Journal Prompt: If you were to allow yourself to receive more, receive help, have more connection, how would your life change?

MY REFLECTION

DATE / /

22 BECOMING THE ALCHEMIST THROUGH RITUALS

WHEN I CREATE RITUALS, IT HELPS ME BECOME MORE PRESENT AND GRATEFUL FOR EACH AND EVERY MOMENT

I'm sitting in my little sacred space drinking a cup of cacao. Mmmm it tastes yummy. I can smell the richness of the cacao. With every sip, I am grateful for this moment and for this drink. I am grateful to be alive and to be having this experience.

———

I love rituals. I love setting intentions and tapping into the energy of the space I am in. There is something so sacred and magical about setting out time for myself and creating a ritual. It can be as simple as a dance, enjoying a cup of cacao, or setting a space or an alter where I can go to anytime I want to connect. I find setting intentions is like creating magic in my life. I don't think I realised it was a ritual experience I was creating in my life until recently.

When I do rituals, I feel so much more present. I feel safe and connected. I really honour the space and time I am giving to myself. Whenever I feel a bit disconnected or lost, I connect to an intention and set up some form of ritual for myself. One of my favourites is making a cup of raw cacao. It feels like medicine for me, I take my time to prepare it, with some music on in the background, and before I drink it I close my eyes and give thanks for the medicine and for it opening up my heart and boosting feel good chemicals throughout my whole body.

I feel that since I've been more intentional through this process, I feel more gratitude for life. I am reminded of how beautiful life is, and how lucky I am to be here experiencing all that I do. I am reminded that all that really matters is the moment I am in. The past is in the past, and the future is yet to unfold. Being more present and more connected in that very moment, and being appreciative of it, will impact what is to come next in my life.

It's interesting to observe it too, because when I do go a bit off track and don't feel as present and a bit lost in the day-to-day errands, I feel more heavy and a bit stuck. So, creating rituals has definitely been a wonderful way of remembering and coming back to this place of ease.

We can create rituals in any form in life.One idea could be to make a hot bath with candles and incense. Or, as mentioned before, create a space in your home that feels really sacred and calm with some of your favourite crystals and essential oils, allow yourself to connect to your senses. It could be as simple as making a cuppa and setting the intention to be present with the drink and to drink it slowly; noticing your surroundings, noticing the taste and noticing the warmth as you drink it.

Rituals help me feel calm and relaxed, away from the busy day-to-day life. They help me to connect more deeply to myself and to remind myself that I am okay, that I am doing my best and that I am enough in each and every moment. It's a reminder that I am worthy and deserving to take that time for myself. By doing so, I continue to raise my vibration and share that energy with everyone I meet throughout my day. As I fill up my own cup first, I can then share the love from that space.

Do: I invite you to create a little space at home where you can create a ritual. It could be as simple as making a cuppa with intention and then being present and grateful whilst enjoying your cuppa within that loving space. Notice how it feels when you give yourself the space and time to do so.

Feel: Are there any areas in your life that's like a ritual? How does that feel for you?

Think: Where in your life do you feel more present and in the moment?

Journal Prompt: Imagine your life is filled with ritual, presence and magic. What would you like to unfold? What does your life look and feel like?

MY REFLECTION

DATE   /   /

23 BEING IN FLOW

WHEN I COME INTO A STATE OF FLOW, I SURRENDER TO LIFE AND ALL IT'S MAGIC

Oh I feel your resistance. I want to take control, but then I remember when I do so I am not in flow. I gently begin to soften into it, and breathe. I am okay. This too shall pass. My body begins to relax again.

Throughout my life, there's been times when I've been in flow and other times when not so much. I've noticed that the more I can allow myself to be in flow, the more at ease I feel. The more I trust life and surrender into the unknown, the more life supports and holds me.

For a long time I didn't know what flow felt like, I was always living in a state of anxiety and fear, that something bad was going to happen and that I wasn't safe. I would resist and hold on to stuff, I would harden myself to protect myself and, by doing so, I'd also shut down my heart. I believe this is also why I started to experience panic attacks - there was such a build-up on my nervous system and the panic attack was like a huge release of energy that I had unnecessarily held onto.

The more I've allowed myself to open, to open my heart to it all, the more I've realised how much love there is and how much more I can be in the flow through adventure, through relationships and through everything else that comes my way. I also feel it's good to have moments where I am not in flow, so that I can feel the difference. It acts as an anchor to get me back into the flow state; if I didn't feel the non-flow state, I'd never know what feeling in flow would be like. It's easy, receptive and blissful. Very like the feminine.

Being in flow is like dancing with life. Dancing with all the experiences, with all the emotions, opening my heart fully to experience it all. Welcoming everything as an invitation to feel more, to be more and to experience more. Flow for me also feels non-linear. There is no end goal, no trying to get somewhere, just enjoying each day as it comes and being in each and every experience.

Do: Can you let go today and just go with the flow? See what may unfold as you do so.

Feel: Can you remember a time where you felt in flow and life felt easy. What were you doing and how did you feel?

Think: If you can allow yourself to be more with the ebbs and flows of life, how would your life change?

Journal Prompt: As you imagine yourself living in a state of flow, or trust, surrender and just be in the magic of it all. How is your life unfolding?

MY REFLECTION   DATE   /   /

24 EMBODIED LIFE

AN EMBODIED LIFE, IS A FULLY LIVED LIFE

Breathe. I tell myself. Take a deep breath. Ahh, there it is. I feel it moving into my arms, my legs, my belly. I feel it moving into my chest and back. With each inhale my body is expanding. With each exhale, my body is relaxing. I feel energy flow. I feel sensations in my body. This is embodiment. Being. Breathing. Experiencing.

Embodiment means to inhabit self. To be connected to the truest and most authentic version of myself and to show up from that space. The embodiment of joy, sadness, pleasure, anger and grief. It's allowing myself to feel and welcome all my emotions. It's about embodying all the parts of myself, including those parts I have disowned, have shame around or don't like about myself. It's about living and leading from my heart.

For a very long time, I was living a life that was from a place of disconnect and disembodiment. Always in my head, always giving my energy externally. I was the last to receive my love. I didn't feel my emotions fully and I definitely had shame around feeling anger. I would allow myself to feel some emotions, the happier ones you could say, and disregard the other emotions. However, by doing, so I wasn't fully living. I wasn't feeling the full spectrum of happiness. Instead it was just a snippet of what I could truly experience.

It wasn't until I was beginning to unravel this disconnect I had with myself, and began to welcome in parts of myself that I didn't like, that I started to feel more and experience more in my life. When I started to lean more into my feminine and into my body, I started to feel more embodied. I could feel my intuition getting stronger. I could feel myself wanting to say no to things that didn't feel right and I began to connect more to my truth and who I am.

Embodiment for me, now, is a way of being and living each and every day. Setting an intention for my day would open with, *How do I want to feel and how can I embody that feeling as I move through my day?*, but that now also includes me embodying the sadness, anger, frustration and anxiety. Not that I would let it fuel my whole day, as my high vibe state is a state of love and fullness, but I allow myself to feel all those things with love.

I've noticed the more I allow myself to feel the emotions as the come, the quicker they pass, the less I resist, the more I feel. It's a daily practice! Being so used to living in a disconnected way for so long, I can still lose myself from time to time, but I feel I have lots of amazing tools that support me and remind me of the importance of feeling all that I feel.

It's also led me to study to become a Feminine Embodiment Coach which I am currently learning to do at the moment. Everything I am learning and reading on I feel like my inside is like, *Yes! This is the way I should be living more often.* We have been living in a very masculine dominated culture which is essentially doing, go-go-go and outward energy. This leaves women feeling fatigued, exhausted and disconnected, including me. But there is another way, the embodied way.

For me, embodiment is also feeling so much more connected to everything around me; nature, relationships, taking a shower, having a cacao, doing dance - allowing myself to be fully in that moment of experience, without thinking of the to-do list or what's going to happen next in my day, week or month. It's a daily practice, for sure, and sometimes I do still get caught in my head, over thinking, but by having more awareness and coming back into the moment, and back into my body, helps me come back to that state and feel connected again and more centred.

Do: I invite you to dance with whatever emotion you are feeling in this moment right now. Play a song that will help you to connect with the emotion and allow your body to move however it wants to move and notice what arises for you.

Feel: Do you feel you live life more from your mind or body? How would it feel to live more from an embodied experience?

Think: What is your current relationship with your body and sensations within your body? Do you find it easy or challenging to go to that place?

Journal Prompt: If you were living a more embodied life, connected to your authentic, truest self, had boundaries in place and knew in every moment what was true for you as you felt so connected to your body's wisdom, how would your life change?

MY REFLECTION   DATE   /   /

25 SURRENDERING TO LIFE
LIFE IS ALWAYS FOR ME, NOT AGAINST ME

Thank you life for being there for me. Even though I am feeling challenged in this moment, I know deep down that you always have my back. There is meaning to this experience right now. I am being taught something, learning something. Thank you for reminding me to trust. I find it hard sometimes, but I know this is all happening for a reason.

Even in the midst of grief, or life's challenges, I am learning more to accept that life is always happening for me. Reminding myself that I chose this life, I chose my life lessons and that everything is unfolding as it should.

I realise that the more I can be with this and surrender to life and all it offers me, the more I can accept what is. It's not easy. Sometimes it's hard and it's painful, sometimes even unbearable. Like moving through grief of my dad I often thought, *Why? Why so young? We didn't have enough time.* My mind running through every scenario. But again I have to soften back into it, allow myself to feel the anger, the sadness, but also the love.

A recent example of when I felt life was for me, was when I was looking for a new place to rent. I had been looking on and off for a few months and I was having a bit of difficulty finding something due to having a dog because a lot of rentals wouldn't accept dogs.

I viewed a few places but nothing came of it. Either I didn't feel it was suitable or I didn't hear back from them. I also had a good idea of what I wanted; I wanted to be close to the beach, in a lovely calm home, and there to be a space within it that I could work and do my daily practices within.

A few months later, I went to see a place in a local town I like. Actually, as I write this I am sitting in the exact coffee shop I sat in just before I went to view my new home. Instantly I liked the vibe in the house when I checked it out and I spoke with the adviser who told me that there had been a lot of interest in the house and that it was down to the owner whom she would choose to rent the place. I put down my interest and was advised that I would know later that day if I had been chosen.

I went home and surrendered to myself that if that home was for me, I would be accepted. A few hours later and received a call from the rental place to inform me that the owner wasn't really fussed on who was taking the rental and had left it to the rental adviser who was calling me. She then informed me that she felt I was the right fit and asked if I want to move forward. I was delighted and trusted that I was meant to take this place and it would be a new beginning for me.

Everything fell into place and I moved in. I absolutely love my new space and feel at ease living there. Every day I'm down at the beach with my dog and feel such gratitude for this space I have now.

I reflected back on other times where I felt challenged with a situation, but actually it was the best thing to happen. For example, a relationship ends and you feel devastated but a few years later you look back and you think, *Wow, I am so glad that happened because look where I am now.* Or a job offer doesn't come through, but then something better comes along after it. Sometimes in the midst of a situation, it can feel like a lot, but I do believe underneath it all is love and we are being taken care of.

SURRENDERING TO LIFE - PRESCRIPTION

Do: If there is a situation in your life where you feel you are holding on and finding it hard to trust the outcome, I invite you to lean into surrender. To connect to your heart and know that life is working for you and that everything you want you already have. To see if you can trust the process a little more.

Feel: Do you find it easy to surrender to the flow of life? How does that feel?

Think: Can you remember a time where you felt challenged and were resisting something, and then when you let go it all worked out? What did you experience?

Journal Prompt: If life is for you, what areas in your life can you give thanks to when you reflect back?

MY REFLECTION   DATE   /   /

THE BEAUTY IN BEING LOST AND FOUND

BEING LOST AND FOUND ARE BOTH GOOD, AND I CHOOSE TO CONTINUE TO LOSE AND FIND MYSELF

Every time I lose myself, it gives me the opportunity to find myself, and when I find myself, I get the opportunity to lose myself again. I dance with life.

As I write this final chapter, the beauty in being lost and found, I reflect back to the start of this journey and where I was at. I felt really lost, uncertain of life and wasn't in a great place, but what the experience gave me was the opportunity to write this book. It started off with me just writing what I was feeling to help me process it all, which has now led to publishing a book.

I sit and feel gratitude for all the times I've been lost and found. For all the times I've felt joy, sadness, pleasure, pain, openness, frustration. This is life. This is all teaching me to live life more fully. Yes, it can be hard, but it can also be wonderful.

So many adventures and experiences. So many 'aha' moments. So many things to let go of. I wouldn't change any of it. I want to dance with life more often, I want to welcome it all in. It will still be scary sometimes and I will always have days where I feel like, *What am I doing?!* But then another moment of, *Everything is good!* Life, hey.

I also feel some sadness as the book comes to an end. This has felt a bit like therapy writing my life's experiences so far and some of it has been very vulnerable to share too. I feel like it's closing a chapter of my life somehow, and that I am letting go of my past. I guess with that I am opening up to something new but I'm not sure what yet. Well, actually, there are some ideas floating around... but I will trust and dance with it.

As I started a small bit of writing that day in Lisbon, little did I know that a book was on its way to being birthed into the world, and now it's in your hands as you read it.

The beauty in being lost and found is that we are always losing and finding ourselves. There is no end goal. No destination. Being lost and found are both good and I will always welcome in more moments of being lost and found through a dance with life. I wouldn't have it any other way.

In what ways can you allow yourself to dance more with life? Let more love in? How would it feel to flow through life with more ease, experiencing the full spectrum of all you feel? I invite you to give it a try.

Dance with me. Dance with life and all her beauty. You have this one precious and beautiful life. Live it fully, live it daringly, and be free.

The End.

Well, for now anyway…

ACKNOWLEDGMENTS

There are so many incredible people who have helped me throughout my journey, and I feel such deep gratitude towards them for being in my life.

My mum and dad, for brining me into this world and all the teachings and learnings I've experienced through them.

My friends over the years for all their support and always being there for me through the highs and lows.

My friends who became my Saudi family, during my few years whilst living and working there and all the amazing experiences we had together.

My amazing coach Jill Ritchie and now lifelong friend, for helping me move through so much especially when I was transitioning back home from Saudi and felt a bit lost and unsure of my future.

My amazing friend and coach Lynette Gray for all her support, her energy and presence is so loving and magnetic.

My grief therapist Kayleigh O'Connor, who helped me so much during the first few tender and vulnerable months of losing my father.

My amazing mentors, Rebecca Wilson and Chelsea Etienne, who helped me embark on my journey of reconnecting to my feminine and doing a lot of healing with my heart and womb, helping me break free the patterns of my lineage and ancestors.

To all those who have worked with me and allowed me to hold sacred space for them and share my wisdom and teachings.

To Sean & Karen and their amazing team at TGH: The Good House, that helped me through bringing this book to life.

And finally, to my guides, seen and unseen who support me and guide me every day, especially those days when life feels a little crazy.

Thank you, thank you, thank you.

ABOUT THE AUTHOR

Samantha is a coach, mentor, facilitator, and reiki master. Through her work, she loves to helping people live and lead through the heart and embody their fullest expression. She holds women's circles, cacao ceremonies and retreats, and loves bringing people together to feel held, heard, and seen, to share stories that remind all of the interconnectedness of each other and life experiences. She also offers 1:1 coaching and mentor support for those who wish to dive deeper on a more intimate space.

When she's not doing the above, she spends time in nature, loves cooking, connecting with friends, enjoying mornings with cacao, planning adventures and having fun with her dog Bear.

You can find out more about her via her website and Instagram links.

www.rootedinlove.co.uk

IG @roootedinlove

Lightning Source UK Ltd.
Milton Keynes UK
UKHW051600270223
417717UK00024B/84